Weaving Wind and Stone

Talks on Zen and Relationships

Leland E. Shields

Jūgum Press
Seattle

Jugum Press
520 Occidental Avenue South #601
Seattle, Washington 98104

ISBN: 979-8988286226
First Edition: November 2024
Find ebook editions at: www.jugumpress.net

Cover art, title page: "Moores Creek 4" (detail),
ink and mixed media on paper, 13.5 x 13.5 inches,
by David Berger (copyright © 2023 by David Berger,
used by permission, https://davidaberger.net)
Book design: Annie Pearson

To Jack Duffy, my teacher and friend of many years. This book exists because of your patient guidance as I stumbled over each rock on the road.

To my wife, Lili, for your support through this project and much, much more.

Although I try
to hold the single thought
of Buddha's teaching in my heart,
I cannot help but hear
the many crickets' voices calling as well.

From *The Ink Dark Moon*

The teacher said, "Don't think good; don't think evil.
At this very moment, what is the original face of
[you, reading now]?"

From *The Gateless Barrier*
[amended]

Contents

Acknowledgments

Many dear friends and fellow travelers on the way have given their time to review drafts and sections so I could clarify and hone. Thanks to Carlos Abusaid, Joe Bobrow, Janise Hurtig, Larry Keil, Lawson Sachter, David Stallings, and Emily Warn.

I first gave each chapter as a talk to the Three Treasures Sangha. My co-teacher Madelon Bolling has been a trusted editor and collaborator on these and all my talks before I presented them. Thanks to all the sangha members for their encouraging and critical feedback on these and all my talks so I can tell how my words are received.

The lovely ink-on-rice-paper cover art is the work of David Berger. I'm grateful for his permission to use it and all his feedback on presentation. I'm grateful also for the design assistance from Rose Goodman.

Without the generous assistance of Annie Pearson, my publisher and editor, you can be sure this project would not be done yet. She understood what I was trying to say and helped craft the words and the feel.

And deep gratitude for all whose stories I've included and whose names were anonymized: your stories have taught me, and it is through them that I've tried to make these writings personal and about all of us.

Under it all, no understanding of relationship could have been possible for me without the love, support, and open-hearted connections with my kids, Eli and Maya, and their families, my siblings, Tony and Lucy, and their families.

Credits for Quoted Material:

Diamond Sangha Sutras. Translated by Robert Aitken. © by Honolulu Diamond Sangha. Used by permission via Honolulu Diamond Sangha correspondence.

Sutra book of the Three Treasures Sangha of the Pacific Northwest (Diamond Sangha lineage). Includes passages from Diamond Sangha Sutra and "Four Infinite Vows," translated by Jack Duffy. Used by permission via correspondence.

Robert Aitken, excerpts from *Encouraging Words: Zen Buddhist Teachings for Western Students* by Robert Aitken, copyright © 1993 by Robert Aitken. Used by permission of Pantheon Books, an imprint of the Knopf Doubleday Publishing Group, a division of Penguin Random House LLC. All rights reserved.

Robert Aitken (translator), excerpts from *The Gateless Barrier: The Wu-Men Kuan.* Copyright © 1990 by Robert Aitken. Reprinted with the permission of North Point Press.

Bashō, excerpts from *Basho: The Complete Haiku,* translated by Jane Reichhold. Copyright © 2013 by Jane Reichhold. Reprinted with the permission of Kodansha International.

Bashō, excerpts from *The Moon in the Pines: Zen Haiku,* selected and translated by Jonathan Clements. Copyright ©

2000. Used by permission from Frances Lincoln Children's Books.

Chao-chou, excerpt from *The Recorded Sayings of Zen Master Joshu,* translated by James Green. Copyright © 2001 by James Green. Reprinted by arrangement with The Permissions Company, LLC on behalf of Shambhala Publications Inc., Boulder, Colorado, shambhala.com.

Eihei Dogen, excerpt from *The True Dharma Eye: Master Dogen's Three Hundred Koans,* translated by Kazuaki Tanahashi and John Daido Loori. Copyright © 2005 by Kazuaki Tanahashi and John Daido Loori. Reprinted by arrangement with The Permissions Company, LLC on behalf of Shambhala Publications Inc., Boulder, Colorado, shambhala.com.

Eihei Dogen, excerpt from Steven Heine, *The Zen Poetry of Dogen: Verses from the Mountain of Eternal Peace.* Copyright © 1997 by Steven Heine. Reprinted with the permission of Steven Heine.

Ikkyū, excerpts from *Crow with No Mouth,* translated by Stephen Berg. Copyright © 2000 by Stephen Berg. Reprinted with the permission of The Permissions Company, LLC on behalf of Copper Canyon Press, coppercanyonpress.org.

Ikkyū, excerpts from "A Gentleman's Wealth" and ["For twenty years I was in a turmoil..."] from *Wild Ways,* translated by John Stevens. Translation copyright © 1995, 2007 by John Stevens. Reprinted with the permission of The Permissions Company, LLC on behalf of behalf of White Pine Press, whitepine.org.

Izumi Shikibu, ["Although I try / to hold the single thought..."] from *The Ink Dark Moon: Love Poems by Ono No Komachi*

Red Pine, excerpts from *Three Zen Sutras.* (New York: Counterpoint, 2021.) Reprinted with the permission of The Permissions Company, LLC on behalf of Counterpoint Press.

Ryokan, "Loneliness" from *One Robe, One Bowl: The Zen Poetry of Ryokan,* translated and introduced by John Stevens, First edition, 1977. Protected by copyright under the terms of the International Copyright Union. Reprinted by arrangement with The Permissions Company, LLC on behalf of Shambhala Publications Inc., Boulder, Colorado, shambhala.com.

Shitou Xiqian, excerpt from "The Tallying of Difference and Sameness," translated by Nelson Foster. Copyright © 2023 by Nelson Foster; used by permission of Nelson Foster.

Stonehouse, #38 ["Scorpion tails and wolf hearts pervade the world"], translated by Red Pine, from *The Mountain Poems of Stonehouse.* Copyright © 1986, 1999, 2009, 2014 by Red Pine. Reprinted with the permission of The Permissions Company, LLC on behalf of Copper Canyon Press, coppercanyonpress.org.

Thich Nhat Hanh, excerpt from "Please Call Me by My True Names" from *Call Me By My True Names: The Collected Poems of Thich Nhat Hanh.* Copyright © 1999 by Unified Buddhist Church. Reprinted with the permission of The Permissions Company, LLC on behalf of Parallax Press, Berkeley, California, www.parallax.org.

Yamada Kōun, Robert Aitken, and Nelson Foster, with revisions and Pinyin transliteration by Michael Kieran, translators, "Case 74: Jinniu's Rice Pail," in *The Blue Cliff Record.* Copyright © 2008 by Honolulu Diamond Sangha. Used by permission via Honolulu Diamond Sangha correspondence with author.

—

Note: For each quotation in *Weaving Wind and Stone,* you can find reference details in "Specific Citations" at the end of this book.

Weaving Wind and Stone
Talks on Zen and Relationships

Introduction

In the historical Buddha's story, he was so compelled to find a way to live in this world of inevitable loss that he separated from his community and his family. He tried many practices without resolution before sitting under the Bodhi Tree for seven days and seven nights and truly seeing the Venus star as it was on the morning of the eighth day. Sometime later he rose and joined his friends.

Stories of our ancestors fashioned into Zen koans have been used for more than a thousand years to aid us in seeing that which there is to see and responding in accord. With every koan, each of us as Buddha has the opportunity to see what is before us. The years and miles that separate us from these ancient stories fall away, and we find ourselves within these ancestors.

This book began with a series of talks that used koans to step into the humanity of interactions. The vitality for the koans discussed lies in the human interaction, the chafing we can't avoid even as we try to separate ourselves through the meditation techniques we hope will protect us.

The lineage in which I study is a lay tradition passed through Jack Duffy, my teacher, Robert Aitken, his teacher and founder of the Diamond Sangha, and Yamada Kōun, Aitken's teacher in Japan.

That worldly grounding helps bring Zen to the lives of us lay folk who know the rub of *that person* at work, *that family member* making it awkward, and the disconnect between our bank balances and bills. Yet in the short time I stayed in a monastery, I didn't see the humanity of interactions there as much different in this regard. It is, perhaps, all the better that our koans are no purer than me, you, and the lives we lead.

The material for this book arose from my own metabolization of this ancient practice into my life of love and loss, peace and discord, which mix poignantly together. I turned it into a book to share with others who are finding their own ways to bring Zen to the unvarnished mess of this one life. While our practice is solitary, koan stories also show that together we are engaged in meaningful ways, with mutual support present in our traditions.

In my day job as a psychotherapist, I have the honor of seeing the timelessness of these ancient stories in another context. I use koans and other stories like myths that collapse the distinctions of millennia and miles. They show undeniably that you and I live in this world of pain and beauty and must navigate at times when all choices are undesirable, if not aversive. When anxiously waiting two weeks for a biopsy report to tell me whether I have cancer, just this. When watching a loved one dying slowly, just this. Separate from Zen training, we all are practitioners of the Way.

This book begins with two koans that pull us out of our pristine quiet and into the humanity we never left, reminding us that there is no one we meet who is not our teacher and who is not the Buddha. The book then highlights the form (observable ritual) of our practice when we are not within the walls of our meditation rooms, asking the question: When we don't have the clear form and guidance of our practice, how do we carry Zen? The chapters that follow pair ancient koans with contemporary stories and poems, and linking them to important and disordered aspects of life and relationships.

Years of practice and the number of koans addressed are not credentials when rubbing against those we live, work, and vote with (and against). This rubbing creates the heat in many of the stories in this book as well.

Whether in retreat, reading a book, or in front of the TV, you and I are under the Bodhi Tree. We care for our bodies with meals, sleep, sitting and walking meditation, and interacting with those around us. Central to our practice, whether in a room of black cushions, in the kitchen over an informal lunch, or joining the cacophony of life, is the letting go of concepts and standing with that which is simply true, not constrained by words.

Yet we are all social creatures. Shame and embarrassment are intense emotions arising from our awareness of others, the need to belong, to be respected, and to be cared for. We also all know what it feels like to be angry, hurt, let down, or mis-

WEAVING WIND AND STONE

understood. We may also feel called to respond to what we see as injustice, exploitation, and mean-spiritedness. Finding ourselves in the old stories and in our lives today, the questions naturally arise: Where is Zen now? For me? Here?

These stories are valuable to me, though some were not immediately so. I've carried them for years and distilled them in talks with students and with others in my life. It was my honor to write this and reflect on my embrace of the stories, dynamics, and questions they stimulate. My hope is that you, as a reader and practitioner, will make each story your own, in your way.

Leland Shields
Seattle, 2024

Everyone we meet is our teacher

Chü-chih and True World

There is a time in our Zen practice when we necessarily settle in the quiet of our zazen meditation, releasing into this one breath, this koan, and this sound. By doing so, we foster our way to meet the world as it is before the imposition of our ideas upon it and ourselves.

Simultaneously, the world comes to us, as we see in the following two koans. The first, Chü-chih and True World, is from a translation by Robert Aitken in *The Gateless Barrier:*

> One day toward evening a nun named [True World] appeared at [Chü-chih's] hut. True World did not knock or call out when she arrived, but just walked in...and there was Chü-chih, sitting in Zazen, right in the center. Without taking off her sedge hat, she walked around him three times and then stood before him saying, "If you can say an appropriate word, I will take off my hat." [She rudely did not follow etiquette by bowing.] Chü-chih was unable to respond. He seemed dumbstruck.

...[Twice more] True World walked around him...,
stood before him, and said, "If you can say an appropriate word, I will take off my hat."... [Each time]
silence. So she turned and walked out. When Chü-
chih finally came to himself, he went to the door after
her and called out, "It will be dark soon. Why don't
you stay the night?" She turned around and said, "If
you can say an appropriate word, I will stay the night."
He still couldn't say a word, so she left.

Chü-chih was downcast. He felt he had been defeated
by True World and thought, "I'm going about this
matter of finding realization the wrong way. I need
a good teacher."...Sure enough, in a couple of days
T'ien-lung appeared.

Chü-chih told him the whole story, and T'ien-lung
raised one finger. With this Chü-chih was enlightened
to the dimensions of the true world.

The second koan is Case 154 from *The Entangling Vines:
A Classic Collection of Zen Koans:*

There was an old woman who supported a hermit. For
twenty years she always had a girl, sixteen or seventeen
years old, take the hermit his food and wait on him.
One day she told the girl to give the monk a close hug
and ask, "What do you feel just now?"

The hermit responded, an old tree on a cold cliff;
Midwinter—no warmth.

The girl went back and told this to the old woman.
The woman said, "For twenty years I've supported this

vulgar good-for-nothing!" So saying, she threw the monk out and burned down the hermitage.

These stories both involve monks who have separated from the world to dedicate themselves to the Way of Zen. Both monks have the world outside their huts intrude upon them, in these cases in the form of women, demanding that their practices include participation with others. Separately and together, they provide opportunities to understand and hone our lay practices.

We are far from ancient China as we read these koans today. The stories use gender roles and hitting that may offend us. Our responses to the images arise from our experiences, and our modern and familial cultures. This too is the intrusion of the world on us now. We don't have to treat others or to teach as the characters in koans do, we can find our own ways. But, if trusting the koans have been passed down because they contain something of value for us now, what do you find? What is the true expression here that can be your expression?

When discussing these stories in other contexts, I focus on their reflection of our personal practices, yours and mine. We can also see through them to engage in the one practice we all share. Chü-chih conceded that he had been unable to respond to True World, and in a sense his own practice let him down—in recognizing his response in accord, he sought more training.

We don't know whether the old-tree–cold-cliff hermit was satisfied with his response. What do you think would have better satisfied the old woman? As a hermit, what is your response?

Zen is a simple, lovely, and sometimes demanding practice. It affords an opportunity to slow our minds and our lives so that we can fully experience the light of day washing across the wood floor in a slow, continuous dance from the east to the west. During a day of meditation, bells ring and we sit. Bells ring and we turn, stand, and walk, playing our own part in the dance with the light, keeping our time as the sun moves, not too fast and not too slow. Our cadence is set with numerous bells and clappers but with few words. Together we move through the day. And individually face the wall, breathe, listen, return to Mu, and practice in the ancient way. Just this. Neither one nor many, just this.

When each in our spaces now, wherever we are, we practice; sharp and dull are part of the dance, focused and dispersed. Eyes open, we receive the light shining off that which is before us.

We have koans and stories in our practice that demonstrate the fundamental experience of the Buddha—just this, in words, in deeds of slaps and simple gestures (like the lifting of one finger). We also have stories that point to a path, paying attention, letting all else fall away. I am grateful for the forms we have, as well, that bring us together on formal days of meditation, sitting many hours in silence. In the silence we have elegant simplicity—each with reactions, expectations, and stories that arise which are undeniably our own. In the near silence of our form, if our attention is drawn to our own regrets or wanderings, there is no other to blame or take responsibility. It is up to each of us individually to find a way to foster falling away. Whatever anyone in the room is doing, each of us has one focus. It may seem that your practice is your own, and mine is my own.

When we leave our dojos, the practice has a different cadence in the give and take of interactions. Even if fundamentally no different, it often seems very different. How do we carry our practice to the fast, interactive world of relationships?

It is essentially the same to carry Zen practice out of a practice center, or even to interact outside our practice halls, as it is with each other in informal times. When we meet each other, our friends, family, and coworkers, there is still only just this, still only attention. Meeting a friend or one with whom we have discord is no different than meeting Master Chao-Chou as he shouts Mu! It is no different than observing T'ien-lung raise his index finger. But we are not in ancient China, so the response must be in accord with each of us, here and now, and in accord with that which is with us.

A magazine article I read years ago comes to mind in reflecting on the one practice we share. The article was written by a musician who wondered how animals related to each other through music. He didn't stop with wondering, though; he also made a practice of it. He took instruments to a place where he knew birds sang at sunrise. He sat under a tree in which a bird was repetitively singing a beautiful song, and he played a couple of instruments, listening to see whether the bird would sing and play with him. Indeed, when he played the flute, the bird began to adapt her song, and they played together for some time. The bird was not just singing independently of the world around her; her song was a part of the whole.

The musician then went to a wildlife preserve one moonlit night and sat down with a fence between him and a pack of wolves baying together. The musician listened a long time before joining his voice to theirs, but when he did, the wolves all immediately stopped baying as if of one voice. He waited through the silence until they began again one at a time, and he listened before he tried his own voice in another way. Again the wolves sharply ceased their song. One sat directly across from him as if to mentor him. The musician repeated his attempts several times until he was able to sing in a way that encouraged the wolves to continue. The musician and wolves together sang for quite some time before all stopped again, one by one, and remained sitting in silence, he on one side of the fence, they on the other. All appeared content, looking at the moon; after a while, the wolves stood and wandered away.

In preparation for a third jam session, the musician made an instrument that floated in the water and that had bars he could strike with mallets to play various notes. The sound resonated though the water as he played. He took this instrument to places where he thought he might find porpoises. Seeing some, he swam out near them. With goggles, he put his head under water so he could see the porpoises, then raised his head to play. The porpoises changed their path to swim in circles around him. Enthralled, he kept playing; the porpoises started breaching all around him, splashing back into the water, as he lifted his head briefly to play and then submerged again to see them swim. After some time, the porpoises continued their original path and swam off.

Whether in a room of black cushions, in the kitchen over an informal lunch, or joining the cacophony of life and relationship, central to our practice is the letting go of concepts and standing with that which simply is, not filtered through words. The musician's story is an example of interactions in relationship without concepts. Acknowledging that I don't know the minds of birds, wolves, and porpoises, I expect that these creatures respond to the world with less of a story of self, past, and future than we do. The musician was not able to join their dance and song on the first try, but he kept listening, and with these various creatures, shared one practice. Just baying. In accord. Of one mind, body, and species.

What does it take to seamlessly join in relationship? In the story of Chü-chih you may conclude that it takes a sharp mind, quick-witted enough that one is never caught without a sage response. Perhaps Chü-chih had that expectation of himself and thus was not able to respond to True World. But T'ien-lung's response, raising one finger, is ordinary. Nothing special. If Chü-chih were not quick-witted and held no concept that he was insufficient for it, he may have returned to his seat after True World left and thought to himself, "Darn, that's so embarrassing that I can't come up with something more quickly." Resting in the truth doesn't mean equanimity as we might wish, but it can include equanimity with embarrassment and awkwardness. That, too, is no-self.

Taking this outside the hut can be even more difficult.

Koans point directly to this fact. Dropping concepts can lead to dropping of distinctions of self and other, like a wave on the ocean. There is no denying that there are individual waves, but where does one start and the other end? One pod of individual porpoises playfully circle, in one motion swimming, breaching, and playing music. There is one voice of flute and bird. One sangha joins in sitting on a gleaming wood floor. And there is one present in an argument with one's spouse, friend, or family member.

So far this sounds comfortable. How welcome would it be to always respond without investment in my image of myself and others' images of me? Our stories and koans often involve interactions with people who don't know each other. Chü-chih had apparently not met True World, and the monk in the hermitage apparently did not have a close relationship with the young woman who brought his food.

By contrast, in our lives today, the deepest challenges to practice often come from those who we know and who are important to us. When present, love can offer a powerful experience of being known and accepted. Love can also include an experience of resting in the truth of what is—this is who I am—and no separation of self and other.

However, any love story I know of, outside a few Disney movies, also includes stumbling over differences and disappointments. At such times it isn't a stranger circling us rudely, it is a colleague doing so repeatedly, wearing us down. Or a spouse, parent, child, old friend, or all of the above.

When someone we have trusted, or need to trust, is disrespectful and critical rather than accepting, they are circling,
asking for a word. In such a moment, you are Chü-chih, with
the knife of the question reaching close to the bone. What
now is your ordinary response?

When your investment in the relationship is deep, or
when the investment in an idea of yourself is central to your
expectations, it is difficult to welcome the truth of what
arises. When the pace is conversational, rather than that of
the path of the sun, it is harder to see more than the momen-
tary impulse. Formal practice no doubt helps us to loosen the
ideas of self in all areas. The story of the hermit and the young
woman warns us that just practicing in isolation may not be
enough. In relationship, it is easier to notice when we have
slipped from the open-handed experience of "we" and my voice
as one indivisible component of a boundless whole, to instead
an experience of "you" and "I" in opposition. But don't worry,
True World will let you know.

In our lives we sometimes have the uncomfortable
experience of meeting not a stranger but someone who is
calling us out on something we did or didn't do. Whether
or not we agree that we transgressed, there are times each
of us inevitably hurts or disappoints someone we care about.
Picture one of these probing encounters in your life:

> You forgot to take out the yard-and-food waste so now
> the house smells like fish. What were you thinking?

> You know how important it is to me to get places on
> time, yet you were forty-five minutes late. If you cared...

How could you drink again after all the family went through before you went to rehab?

What's the point; I just wish I would die.

I want a divorce!

Or perhaps someone you care most about tells you how you let her down, or how furious you are that she let you down. I suspect that lifting a finger would not be well received as a response in many instances. If you settle into the encounter and allow all ideas that anything should be otherwise to fall away, what then is your ordinary response? Take raising one finger not as a response to repeat in a perfunctory way but as a demonstration of acting with immediacy, simply and directly. Perhaps something like, "I'm so hurt I don't know what to say." Or weeping. But only these if words or tears express what is true for you and in accord with where you are. Lighting a match to see may be a perfectly valid choice when you truly need light, but it is still an unfortunate one if you are standing in a dusty coal mine. Or your genuine response may be to dance the tango in 2/4 time; but doing so when the band is playing a waltz in 3/4 time is likely not in accord. So, what is your response to the band? Expanding one's attention to include the world in which one abides dissolves the separation of inside and outside. There is no appropriate response in isolation.

Taking it further, we can also say there is no isolation possible.

I heard of a Zen teacher who counseled that whoever and whatever we encounter we can say, "This too is me." A client gave the phrase to me, from his teacher years before. I found it helpful and so pass it on to you. The expression from that (unknown) teacher is another example of the ways our responses to the world are more than solely our own; they join the totality in ways we may never realize.

Now, fully attending to the one with whom you are arguing and to your own hurt feelings allows the ideas you hold about who you are, who with, and where you are to fall away. Now, there is just the truth of who you are in this moment, whether or not it fits with who you wish you were.

This too is me.

Now there is just the truth of who your loved one is, however either of you feel about that.

This too is me.

Now, there is the room in which you are sitting, perhaps with others around, perhaps with your fatigue from a long day and tasks yet to be done. What is your response? In this case, it could include first sitting down with a sigh.

This too is me.

Returning to the koans of Chü-chih and the old-tree–cold-cliff hermit, we could also describe each as holding back rather than responding fully. We can see another way to respond to the world outside our "huts" is to hold nothing back, act with nothing left. Acting with nothing left can still be simple, such as a bow with body and mind. To try this out, when you're done reading for now, put down the book and stand without leaving your seat.

There is a seeming contradiction that often comes up when we talk about a full and genuine response. I could walk into any bar downtown and, before waiting too long, probably observe someone who was acting less restrained than they were several drinks earlier in the day, ready to express anger without holding back. And that anger may be quite genuine. So why bother with all this sitting if we could act irresponsibly by drinking instead? This is not the same for two reasons. One is that our representative drinker is likely to be very self-engaged and not as likely to be embedded into and in accord with the room and others in it. The second is that acting to protect a limited self is not the same as acting fully. When we are hurt and defensive, it is very difficult to point to that in ourselves which we wish to defend, and say, "This too is me."

Whether recognizing it or not, we cannot separate ourselves from the one dance we all share. We live it now, joining with each gesture, breath, and word.

2
The form of Zen in relationship

Attention. Attention. Attention.

Venerable master Ikkyū (also known as Master Ichu in other sources) was an irascible and irreverent fifteenth-century Japanese teacher who we will get to know better later. Here he offers advice so simple, the student didn't recognize it:

> ...[A] student said to Master [Ikkyū], "Please write for me something of great wisdom." Master [Ikkyū] picked up his brush and wrote one word: "Attention." The student said, "Is that all?" The master wrote, "Attention. Attention." The student became irritable. "That doesn't seem profound or subtle to me." In response, Master [Ikkyū] wrote simply, "Attention. Attention. Attention." In frustration, the student demanded, "What does this word 'attention' mean?" Master [Ikkyū] replied, "Attention means attention."

The previous chapter emphasizes the aspects of koans pointing directly to the fact, without concepts like self and other, to address this one practice we all share. The influential Chinese teacher Linji (also known as Lin-chi) described his own as "exhaustive investigation." Or, we can simply say, "Attention." This chapter will consider the form of our practice in the context of the inevitable heat of interaction with others. Before returning to Master Ikkyū's attention, I'd like to say a few words about why I want to talk about Zen and relationship, then bring in relevant consideration of form, come back to attention, and tie both form and attention to practice in relationship.

The more we are invested, the more we are inclined to fear loss of what we so value. With fear, we tend to contract our attention to focus on protection of what is important to us. Most of us want, if not crave, love, belonging, and respect in many ways, and in many kinds of relationships. And because we each have our own foibles and ways of expressing ourselves and interpreting others, there are moments when our needs are in competition with those of others. At those times, we are each inclined to want others to recognize our perspective, and of course others should see why we are right. Thus, relationship offers a perfect time for practice of attention so that we can open ourselves to all that is present, whether we call it "self" or "other," and release concepts of who is right or wrong.

Attention can be considered as a form for our practice. Form in the dojo is known; with modern adaptations, we follow the ancient way. Form is the container within which we can release considerations extra to these circumstances. While sitting, there is no need to expend any effort to decide whether I'm going to get up and eat potato chips: Now is not the time; that choice was made when I entered the room. Form is also not separate from the experience of the Buddha. Bowing at the period's end is part of our form and at once not separate from the resonance of the bell, or the bow of the followers of the Way to the right and left. We know what to do, from weeks or years of doing it. In Three Treasures Sangha of the Pacific Northwest, we even have a document titled "Dojo Procedures" that presents the form in perhaps obsessive detail.

We have no such document for practice in relationship, though we can extrapolate. While engaged in formal sitting, we bring our attention to the practice, you to yours, and me to mine, whether that relates to this breath, a koan, a sound, or a question such as "Who hears?" While cooking, we bring our attention to chopping, washing, stirring, and tasting. Attention in the kitchen is open. Getting lost in the chopping might mean scorching what is in the pan on the stove. So, our attention includes all that is appropriate. What is appropriate will likely exclude some things as well. When talking to someone in the passenger seat while driving, it is appropriate to notice the response of ourselves and that person; it would be most unfortunate to leave out noticing the other cars on the road and traffic signals.

Because we don't have a document in the Three Treasures Sangha files titled "Relationship Procedures," and we don't have an ancient way that offers guidance about related mindful rituals, the form is one we can create together. Even though I'm writing these words, my role as teacher does not award me unquestioned authority to speak about this subject. There have been too many teachers and leaders in all religions who acted inappropriately in their relationships for us to trust even beloved guides without also attending to the hair when it stands up on the back of our own necks. I instead offer my thoughts to the discussion, while over time, we in the Zen community may explore together the personal and shared forms of our practice in the world.

There is a great freedom in Master Ikkyū's teaching. Attention is enough. We come to the dojo with an intention to focus. We apply ourselves by engaging with our breath, our koan, with this sound. In the dojo we can more often have clarity regarding "attention means attention." When we are sitting diligently on our cushion and start to smell lunch in the next room, what might arise is hunger. So far, so good. We have all sat long enough to know what might next arise: "I wonder what's for lunch." Then, "Damn, when is she going to ring the bell?" And perhaps, "Maybe I'll pick up something for dinner on the way home." And off we go.

At some point we stop…returning to breath as our expression of attention befitting this moment. It is not hard to distinguish food shopping reveries from attention to breath. Granted, this is not the whole picture either. Yes, I can attend to my breathing and by so doing start to slow down, shedding anything extra and finding my way to breath. Yet even saying it the way I did implies something extra. I may begin by experiencing breath and one who is breathing; there is no denying any aspect of this. At the same time, opening completely to stomach growling and mind wandering, without awareness of anyone attending, attention becomes an expression of one state. But I don't know anyone who always rests in the experience of one state. Thus, we have form and practice to support us.

Attention does not require forcefulness; it allows receptivity. These words now are an opportunity for receptiveness, not because what I have to say is so important; but as receptivity practice, it is without effort. Attention is not about expecting to understand; it's about taking it all in, which might include, "I don't get what he's saying." No judgment is needed. In fact, reading or listening to this talk would fit neatly into the theme of attention as a practice in relationship. It is up to us together to come to understanding. In the spirit of simplicity, there is no need to take this *attention* as if it is written in all capital letters or highlighted by a ring of fire. It is enough to notice what is here. Though we may be seduced into making something of this attention, it remains simple.

Attention is not just an expression toward a goal; the practice is the goal itself, as in a poem by Izumi Shikibu from eleventh-century Japan, as translated by Jane Hirshfield in *The Ink Dark Moon:*

> Although I try
> to hold the single thought
> of Buddha's teaching in my heart,
> I cannot help but hear
> the many crickets' voices calling as well.

Even in a luxuriously simple dojo, where all is carefully chosen to support practice, there is the formal practice that helps guide us, and there are songs of the horns, tires, and engines calling us—nothing extra, nothing left out. There is no conflict or discord between Ikkyū's teaching and the full recognition of this breath, as long as our attention is without limits to anything that is.

To communicate this point further, I offer a couple more perspectives, starting with a poem by Li Po, from eighth-century China:

> The birds have vanished down the sky.
> Now the last cloud drains away.
>
> We sit together, the mountain and me,
> until only the mountain remains.

And here, from seventeenth-century Japan, Hattori Toho, a student of the wonderful poet Bashō, first quoted his old teacher and then explained the meaning with respect to writing poetry:

> "Learn about the pine from the pine, learn about the bamboo from the bamboo." This dictum of our teacher means that you must forgo your subjectivity. If you interpret "learn" in your own way, you will end up not learning. To "learn" here means to enter the object; then if its essence reveals itself and moves you, you may come up with a verse.

Izumi Shikibu, Li Po, Bashō, and Hattori Toho all demonstrate how attention can involve not two. These examples also reflect both taking due time and attending to what is present now. However useful these concepts of form and practice can be, by their application we release them. Each time we engage with form—in this case, attention—we may start sitting *with* the mountain; letting everything else fall away leaves *only* mountain. According to Bashō, encounter the object; encounter what arises. Yet there is still room for discernment. If Li Po were to become hypothermic sitting with mountain, I hope he'd attend instead to the chill.

In the west, it is no different. What was Monet doing when he painted stacks of wheat and the Waterloo Bridge over and over, if not entering the object? And what of the painters over the centuries, sitting together with the Grand Canal in Venice?

All these examples are similar to sitting together in the dojo, taking time, settling in. Just as Monet can pull out another canvas for another time of day, the bell rings and we sit together, following the schedule, with and being attention.

Let me return to the practice of listening and reading as an opportunity for receptivity. Whenever listening to others, it is easy to think about what you do or don't agree with, what words you would say, or whether you're engaged or only waiting for me to get to the point. Even if those responses are valid, open attention includes not just your response but also listening for what is true for the speaker. What is the path of your mind as you read? Are you receptive, as fitting to these very circumstances?

Outside the dojo and with others, it is clear that interest in opening to all is not restricted to Zen. There was a scene related to this topic in the play *Elephant Man* that so moved me it is engraved in my mind. If you are not familiar with the story, it is about John Merrick, a horribly deformed English-

man in the late nineteenth century. Deformations of his face
were such that he could not express emotion and his speech
was difficult to understand without practice. We know of
Merrick because of the reflections and memoirs of his doctor,
Sir Fredrick Treves.

In the fictionalized play, Merrick is hospitalized and
under treatment by Treves, who recognized the loneliness
and isolation of the intelligent and sensitive Merrick. Treves
brought in a series of people of different backgrounds to interact
with Merrick. Even seasoned and hardened nurses carrying in
his lunch dropped his tray and screamed, running out. So,
Treves found a talented and famous actress, Mrs. Kendall,
who he thought could act through the meeting rather than
react to Merrick. When I saw the play, the actor playing Merrick was present and genuine, while the actor playing Mrs.
Kendall began with a condescending tone. They speak of books;
he was at that time reading *Romeo and Juliet;* she had played
Juliet and knew the part by heart. The following is taken
from the script at that point. The notes in brackets indicate a
missing subject or are my description of how it seemed to me
the lines were delivered:

> Merrick: ...[Romeo] does not care for Juliet.
>
> Mrs. Kendall: Not care? [With an incredulous tone.]
>
> Merrick: Does he take her pulse? Does he get a doctor?
> Does he make sure? No. He kills himself. The illusion
> fools him because he does not care for her. He only
> cares about himself. If I had been Romeo, we would
> have got away.

Mrs. Kendall: But then there would be no play, Mr. Merrick. [Still with a condescending tone.]

Merrick: If he did not love her, why should there be a play?...That is not love. It was all an illusion. When the illusion ended he had to kill himself.

Mrs. Kendall: Why. That is extraordinary. [Her voice now soft, words slow, thoughtful.]

Merrick: Before I spoke with people, I did not think of all these things because there was no one to bother to think them for. Now things just come out of my mouth which are true.

Mrs. Kendall: [To Treves] Fredrick, I feel Mr. Merrick would benefit by even more company than you provide... Mr. Merrick, it has been a great pleasure to make your acquaintance.

Treves: John. Your hand. She wishes to shake your hand...

This is an extreme example but is reflective of the common challenges we have in relationship all the time. The focus of attention for Romeo was not given. There was not a rule, like breath, to return to. Who could argue with his focus on grief, anger, injustice, retribution, or more? What about attention to Juliet? The scene in *Elephant Man* mirrors the question about Shakespeare's characters too. Mrs. Kendall was dismissive of Merrick, shocked and horrified by his appearance, unable to imagine humanity housed within it. At first her demeanor demonstrated her presumption that this ugly and isolated man could know nothing of love. But she listened; she heard his words, and he was no longer an animal with whom she had nothing in common. She stopped and knew the man. The hospital fell away, the doctor making the introduction was forgotten. How could she help but utter those words, "Why, that is most extraordinary."

Both of these plays—*Romeo and Juliet* and *Elephant Man*—show us viscerally the depth of attachment in relationship. What better place for practice? Recognizing that *Elephant Man* is fiction, I nonetheless value through the resonance within me that there's relevance to the story. For both Merrick and Kendall, attention meant attention; there was no need for explicitly articulated definitions.

Every day, in our own lives, we brush by a myriad of people and things, casually and intimately. I know people who found that very experience in crowded India so painful they ended after one day what was to be a long trip. The recognition of obvious suffering was too much to bear. Perhaps to force oneself to bear the unbearable would be like forcing oneself to sit cross-legged so long that one's body is damaged, or to focus on a formal practice to the exclusion of what is. It would not be for me to evaluate the discernment for these travelers to India. More commonly, we all know times we choose something other than being present with anyone or other than someone in particular. This too is discernment, requiring our recognition of that focus of our attention which is in accord.

So far, I've been setting up the more specific question that I want us to address together. Every day, with the people in your life, and for me in mine, what is Zen practice? It would be limiting to relegate practice to the cushion, when as lay folks we live in the world with others. Is it not our responsibility to show up in the marketplace with gift-bestowing hands? Abraham Lincoln wrote, "I care not for a man's religion whose dog and cat are not the better for it."

Speaking for myself, bringing practice to relationship is not a matter of obligation or belief, but the inexorable direction to which I'm drawn. If you are drawn in another direction, do not be distracted by what I say—though perhaps you will find something of how I let my feet find my way that will also apply to you on yours.

Even if you also are drawn to bring form to your practice in the world, there may be many ways to do so. The Buddha Way is not exclusive. How could it be so when central to it is the simple and unqualified statement, "All beings are Buddha"? This fundamental understanding is inherent in Master Ikkyū's "Attention." With open attention, all else will follow, including discernment of what is attended to, what actions are taken, and the falling away of the person who is attending.

This is not to say that we should presume that right or ethical action is automatic. We find the Middle Way, with neither asceticism nor indulgence. In this case, whether in our own formal practice or relationally, we might say the Middle Way of attention lies between rigidity and laxness.

Being indulgent is not hard to imagine either. If I was enjoying the music through my ear buds, did it matter to you that I swung open my car door and dented your car? And in relationship, the Middle Way is open to all that is, including focus on that which is central, and abandoning with discernment that which is peripheral to what is present. Such open attention calls for courage to observe what may be surprising, inconvenient, or abhorrent.

There is another illustrative story closer to the lives we live every day. This one was told to me by someone I know who happens to have a sitting practice, though that is not essential to the events. One qualification: You will notice that I'm including details about the experiences of people that I'm inferring but don't know to be true for them. Though the story is based on one told to me, the details may as well be fictional. No matter, it is only useful if there is some application to you in your experiences.

A woman I'll call Kate called her mother on speaker phone to say hello. With a derisive tone, her mother referenced Kate's new boyfriend, who I'll call Bill. Kate said, "He's right here, Mom." Kate's mother, again with a critical tone, said Kate never had her mother or father over to the new house. Without mentioning that her mother and father had been invited but had cancelled several times, Kate simply acknowledged it was true. The call went on for a few more similar exchanges. After Kate hung up, Bill began to offer advice about the strained tone Kate had during the call. At that point, Kate became very upset. The two of them found ways to express what their unstated experiences were. For Kate, she had made the call expecting to be judged by her mother but wanted Bill to have contact with her family. If not for him, she wouldn't have called at all. Bill was trying to help by offering his comment. Kate feared the loss of love and connection with Bill, due to his having seen that in the call Kate could not muster anything more open or patient towards her mother than the restrained anger she demonstrated.

How can we bring the practice of attention to this exchange, involving three people, each with their own perspectives and responses? The first is in Kate's decision to call. There are times we know that getting in the strong current of a river has a good chance of taking us crashing over the falls. In such cases there are several choices. One would be to avoid the stream all together—that is, Kate not calling or having contact, and instead Kate caring for herself and accepting the losses of connection and of offering her family to Bill. Another choice would be to get in the river and accept the crash.

Kate acted on her wish to offer family to Bill and accepted once again receiving her mother's judgment. Kate also accepted showing Bill her limit in controlling anger. Attention before the call is fully taking all this in—self, mother, Bill—with open hands and allowing the response to arise. Without attention, it is easier for any of us to be resentful of others for the consequences of our decisions to make such calls.

Attention during the call allows open hands in noticing that which is: Kate's mother expressing disappointment and perhaps resentment; Bill noticing the unrestrained and restrained resentments of Kate and her mother; and Kate feeling unable to avoid her own frustration while wanting to satisfy her mother and Bill. Attention leads to responses, such as

Kate not biting the hook her mother offered about invitations to have the parents visit. Kate did not respond defensively about the history of invitations; she simply acknowledged that they had not visited.

After Kate hung up, for her attention meant allowing with open hands the awareness that she disappointed her boyfriend, plus her own repeated disappointment in her relationship with her mother and in herself for her limits in managing it. Bringing attention is bringing response—not separate from response. For Bill, if his attention was narrow after the call, he would have tried to clarify what he meant and perhaps felt misunderstood. His attention instead opened and included Kate, and so a response rose that was understanding and supportive of her.

Another example arises every day between parents and children. A father asks a teen to clean up his mess. With narrow attention, both strive for their own way, leading to harsh words, slammed doors, and anger all around. Open attention can bring to light the teen chafing at being dominated and also to the father's need for love and respect offended when dismissed. Open attention is intimacy.

Attention is not another project to take on. Just as we don't need to use force to taste—our tongues know what to do—with a broad openness to receive what is and releasing other distractions, we avail ourselves of what is. We pay attention with the simplicity of a child stacking blocks, not noticing that her tongue is sticking out the side of her mouth, leaving only blocks.

At each moment we can bring a quality of attention as we do for this breath while in the dojo. There is no need to measure our attention with words like "full," just as there is no need to measure our breath. In fact, the measuring detracts. Whatever came before, now is opportunity—right here. When interacting with others, we cannot help but lose receptivity due to the tenderness of our own humanity. The more entrenched we are in our own perspective alone, the more tender the feelings must be that we are trying to protect. Sitting in the complete mess of tenderness, right here, attention is attention, gently, receptively.

Revisiting the story of Ikkyū and the student again, it contains an example of attention in relationship in the manner we've been speaking of it. The student asked for great wisdom and received a one-word answer: Attention. Asking again and receiving the same answer evoked frustration and disappointment. To the student's credit, they persevered in keeping awareness of their own yearning. Ikkyū's repetition called the student to release any preconceptions of what is wisdom, and to listen.

Is there anyone who speaks to us who is not Ikkyū, calling us to release preconceptions and listen? In this way, meeting with others in our lives is not something we bring our practice to. Rather, meeting with others, with attention, is Zen practice itself.

3

Contemplation and engagement are not separate

The ceaselessly seeking mind

Let me tell again the central story about the Buddha's life that
contains the originating myth of the times of intensive practice
in Zen called sesshin. It goes like this:

> Driven to find how to live in this world of sickness and
> inescapable loss, Siddhartha spent years searching in all
> ways available among the teachers and seekers of his
> time. He sat with great will and the belief that spiritual
> sustenance was possible while denying the body. After
> years of effort, with his strength failing him, still he
> remained unsatisfied. A woman taking milk to market
> saw Siddhartha and made a compassionate offering of
> milk. Realizing that weakening the body hindered his
> way on the path, Siddhartha accepted milk and regained
> strength. For this perceived indulgence, Siddhartha
> was rejected by his community of seekers. Undeterred,
> he placed a grass mat under the Bodhi Tree and sat
> down, focusing with determination.

The myth in our Zen tradition is that Buddha sat steadfast, seven days and seven nights, beset by the temptations of Mara, the personification of delusion. When seeing the Venus star on the morning of the eighth day, Buddha was awakened. He then rose and proceeded to the city of Sarnath to deliver his first teaching.

Nothing is said about Buddha rising within that seven days to beg for food, drink water, and find a toilet. Having foregone denial of his body, the Middle Way is inferred. I fully trust Siddhartha included care for his body in the days and nights, just as I trust the clear commitment to a quiet mind and sitting without movement.

Whether in retreat, reading a book, or in front of the TV, you and I are under the Bodhi Tree. We too care for our bodies with meals, sleep, sitting and walking meditation, and interacting as fitting with those around us. As we do so, we act on our commitment to being awake by setting aside distractions as we are able, even while caring for our bodies and those around us.

Retreats are designed as settings in which we express our inspiration to practice in luxurious blocks of time that are only available because we've reduced other commitments and activities. In our non-residential sesshin, our contact with the world and other people is a greater part of the week than for our residential sesshin.

There is also no sesshin without Mara because Mara is not separate from us. Mara shows up in the second of the Four Infinite Vows:

Blind passions without cease, I vow to see through.

In the hours of our zazen, Mara is an intimate partner, sometimes referred to as distraction.

The *Merriam-Webster Dictionary* defines distraction as "...an object that directs one's attention away from something else." The *Oxford English Dictionary* gives its etymology from the Latin as "A drawing or being drawn asunder; pulling asunder; forcible disruption, division, or severance."

It seems we can find ways to become distracted even by the question as to what is a distraction. Is it a distraction to be concerned about climate change while sitting and wondering if zazen is the best use of time and energy in this troubled world? In place of climate change, fill in with the personal or world trouble that comes to your mind as we sit.

Distraction and the nature of mind are such that, while engaged in social action, we may wonder if that time would be better used supporting an ill or distressed loved one. And while caring for a loved one, we may wonder if we should be spending more time in meditation. These are all good questions, and priorities are set by our actions every day. Part of our zazen is to quiet the waters of the mind such that a fitting response to those questions is available to us.

Siddartha expressed priorities when leaving a spouse and child at home to begin his search. Frankly, I am troubled by that part of the story, having chosen otherwise when I had a baby in my own home. But I have to presume that Siddartha had to take the one path he took, to the benefit of us all over the last 2,500 years. I cannot know what path would have been best for Siddhartha nor anyone else. I trust you and me each to navigate our way, blundering around in the dark as we do, correcting course when encountering our own discord. Discord calls us to consider whether our blundering fits us personally and morally.

Siddartha chose a path again after seeing the Venus star on the morning of the eighth day; he left his seat to offer new perspective to the friends of his practice community. Seeing him, they immediately knew there was a change and embraced him again. The story shows that sitting does not preclude engagement in the world—each engagement in its time.

With these considerations, I've circled around the use of seclusion to foster deep engagement in practice. As in other faith traditions, Buddhism has a long history of monastic settings, with ancestors spending time in hermitages and with having times of isolated focus. Buddha left home and eventually sat for an extended time alone under this Bodhi Tree. Moses was herding alone for an untold time when he met the burning bush. Jesus went into the desert for forty days and forty nights. In the book, *Thoughts in Solitude,* Thomas Merton wrote:

> If our life is poured out in useless words, we will never hear anything, will never become anything, and, in the end, because we have said everything before we had anything to say, we shall be left speechless.

Merton apparently did not see solitude as separate from action in the world. In his notes from 1953–1954, he wrote:

> I make monastic silence a protest against the lies of politicians, propagandists, and agitators...

Speaking as a lay practitioner, I find that externally manifesting seclusion is a wonderful tool when sitting for an hour or a week, but it is not the final point. Instead, we can use retreats as affirmatively stepping toward receptive silence and as support for receptivity to carry at all times. Carrying the silence with us is the metaphor of Buddha walking away from the Bodhi Tree to meet his friends and speaking.

In the opening paragraph of the Buddha's words as recorded in the Diamond Sutra, the Buddha's presentation of his teaching is clear before he utters a word. Here is Red Pine's translation from *Three Zen Sutras:*

> One day before noon, the Bhagavan put on his patched robe, picked up his bowl, and entered the capital of Śravasti for offerings. After begging for food in the city and eating his meal of rice, he returned from his daily round in the afternoon, put his robe and bowl away, washed his feet, and sat down on his appointed seat. After crossing his legs and adjusting his body, he turned his awareness to what was before him.

Buddha's comportment in the world—going to work— is articulate and complete, offering all that needs to be said. Returning home, he turns his attention to what is before him; "before" carries two meanings: In front of him and through all time until now. In the subsequent paragraphs, as translated in *Three Zen Sutras,* the monks who come for teaching follow suit:

> A number of monks then came up to where the Bhagavan was sitting. After touching their heads to his feet,

39

they walked around him to the right three times and
sat down to one side.

In the next couple of paragraphs of the Diamond Sutra
that come after this passage, there are questions asked of Buddha
to which he responds. Pausing here, notice that these monks
have spoken to us. Take it all, whether you are listening to one
who answers to the name "Buddha," to your name, or to that
of the one whom you find most annoying. Take it in.

To perceive isolation and silence too literally is to experience the world we meet as distraction. We can take the coughing of a person nearby as inhibiting meditation, and we can
take fear of recession and our finances as disrupting our attention. Would you see the choices for your life differently if
distraction is defined as that which pulls our attention from
the present, severing our recognition of nonduality?

Distraction in this way can occur when grasping and when
rejecting the coughing sound. What is it to be present when
the coughing sound dominates over timing bells and birds?

In the Jewish tradition, Satan is not thought of as evil.
Writing in the twelfth century, the Jewish theologian Maimonides said the name Satan is derived from a root meaning "turn
away." Jewish texts often translate Satan as obstruction or
adversary. All these allude to the questions: Turn away from
what? Obstruct from what?

Whether sitting in a Zen center or a home dojo, we all
know the call to turn away. That call can derive from the petty
to the profound—from craving a strawberry to sending a get-
out-the-vote post card. The call to turn away while in the

world is also familiar—having dinner with someone while watching the clock for a work deadline or for the start of the next sitting period.

The commonality of obstruction in faith traditions encourages me: This is not my failing, not your failing; it is life. If this is life, this too is a chance to turn toward.

Returning to our Zen tradition, Linji is recorded as saying this to his community:

> Bring to rest the thoughts of the ceaselessly seeking mind, and you'll not differ from the patriarch-buddha. Do you want to know the patriarch-buddha? He is none other than you who stand before me listening to my discourse. But because you students lack faith in yourselves, you run around seeking something outside. Even if through seeking you find something, that something will be nothing more than fancy descriptions in written words; never would you gain the mind of the living patriarch.

The first phrase in this quote is "Bring to rest the thoughts of the ceaselessly seeking mind..." It would carry a different meaning if Linji left out the word "seeking" and instead said, "Bring to rest the thoughts of the ceaseless...mind..." By suggesting we bring the seeking mind to rest, Linji is encouraging us to have a seat right here, without seeking beyond this place, which includes the ceaseless mind of sense perceptions, thoughts, and feelings. Right here is a place of both contemplation and engagement. As the concise two-thousand-year-old teaching in the Heart Sutra encourages us:

Since there is nothing to attain,
the Bodhisattva lives by Prajna Paramita,
with no hindrance in the mind;
no hindrance and therefore no fear;
far beyond delusive thinking, right here is Nirvana.

The translator of the quote from Linji, using language of
the patriarchy, was Ruth F. Sasaki, who was born in 1892, a
female pioneer of Zen in the West. She was the first foreigner
to be a priest of a Rinzai temple in Japan, and the only woman
and only foreigner to be a priest of Daitoku-ji (at least as of
2006). Encountering phrases like "the patriarch-buddha," our
minds today may naturally find associations with current
questions of language as being inclusive or divisive. That is
the nature of mind. Once such an association arises during
sesshin, now what? Where is the nondual in this moment and
what is hindrance? I'm not offering an answer because you
already have yours or you know how to recognize it.

There was a time for Buddha to sit receptive and a time
to rise and speak. Neither is right or wrong. One is in accord
for this moment. Whether receptive or speaking, can you turn
towards the Tao that dances in all sensations, feelings, and
thoughts in this very moment?

As I wrote this, I recalled a teaching of Eido Shimano
that I can still picture him delivering. At Dai Bosatsu Zendo,
at the end of the meal, we passed teapots down the long table
for use in cleaning our personal set of nested bowls (oryoki
bowls). The teapots were passed on one side only. If I were on
the side that received the pot, holding the handle with two

hands, we would bow and I would offer tea to the person across from me, pour my own, and then pass the pot to the next person. Eido admonished us that when we are offered tea, to take a mindful bow before offering our bowl left the one holding a heavy pot with arms outstretched, waiting uncomfortably. He reminded us that to be sincere and perfect in our form at the expense of another was not in keeping with compassion and not in accord with others. This was deeply meaningful to me as a reminder that the form of practice itself could be a barrier to acting in accord if we are not watchful.

Herein is a koan which is presented to each of us frequently. The awareness of the heavy pot may be straightforward enough. But how often do we have to choose between engaging in the ritual of practice by attending a formal sitting event of hours or days rather than eschewing the ritual and cancelling our retreat plan in order to support a loved one in crisis? And what if it isn't a crisis, but on a spectrum of need?

Returning to Eido, when I later learned that my beloved teacher was causing harm to women students he slept with, I was reminded even more deeply to bring humility to how I considered what was possible through practice. Even while returning to the marketplace with "bliss-bestowing hands," none are immune to being wrong and failing to act in accord. Most importantly, we may not know it when we do.

Still, if not taking Zen as a protection from error, we can use the experiences and principles of our practice, on the cushion and off. There is no end to ways we can be distracted from the action in accord. There is no end to error, and so there is no end to the calls that we open here, and once again.

The truth is that you already know what constitutes a distraction. It's a bit simpler when we have all brought body and mind to sesshin. There may be some of the non-formal times during a sesshin when you can wonder how to express your practice, but I trust we all carry the intention of turning away from the discursive mind for the duration of the sesshin and toward the Tao that also includes maybe this and maybe that. Every one of us has spread out a grass mat, sitting on it under branches and leaves, surrounded by weeds. Together with all, we sit.

In *Cultivating the Empty Field,* we can read the writings of the twelfth-century Chinese teacher Hongzhi (also known as Cheng-chüeh in some sources):

> So nowadays please do not acquiesce to sages and exalt their worth [instead of realizing it yourself]. This is how you should wear the robe and eat your food. When constantly mindful with no distracting considerations, minds do not allow contaminating attachments... Comprehend your sense-object faculties until they are exhausted from top to bottom...Naturally the mind flowers and radiance shines forth, responding to the visible lands and fields. How could you have ever separated from the various permutations? Now you can enter among diverse beings and travel the bird's way without hindrance, free at last.

The line "Comprehend your sense-object faculties until they are exhausted from top to bottom" reiterates Bashō's instruction that to learn about the pine, we have to enter the pine.

When we meditate, work, garden, and converse, we can easily turn away from the singular presence of breath, noise, deadline stress, sun, snails, and the furrowed brow of the one to whom we are speaking. We turn away from the Venus star that is never missing. We can also turn toward breath, noise, deadline stress, and the myriad forms perceptible just now. The Venus star is yours, though it may be known by other names.

This "Song of Zazen" is yours too, from Hakuin Zenji, the influential eighteenth-century Japanese teacher:

> truly is anything missing now?
> Nirvana is right here, before our eyes,
> this very place is the Lotus Land,
> This very body the Buddha.

I have deep respect for the wisdom that leads each of us to take time for zazen and for retreat attendance. I don't need to know the details to trust it; I know it's not a choice casually made. We dedicate precious time to recognize that there's no need to run around or seek outside. It takes dedication and commitment to use *this* time to stop seeking anywhere.

I'll end this chapter with a verse from the fourteenth-century Japanese teacher Keizan, encouraging us to embrace that which is our practice as it is, whether in the autumn of falling leaves or in the spring of wild growth:

Though there be the purity of the autumn waters
Extending to the horizon,
How does that compare with the haziness
Of a spring night's moon?
Most people want clear purity,
But though you sweep and sweep,
The mind is not yet emptied.

4
Hermits and householders

Splash in the mire

In the end of the third century CE, historical sources documented the prominent place of Buddhist and mostly Taoist hermits in the culture of China. Although it appears that hermits long preceded this period, the book *Road to Heaven* summarizes the way of hermits of the later Han dynasty (206 BCE to 220 CE) like this:

> Some retired to achieve their ideals; some bowed out to maintain their principles; some chose quiet to still their passions; some chose escape to preserve their lives; some to shame others into changing their ways; some to cleanse themselves.

These hermits are diverse, some going towards something of promise, some fleeing what they've left, some motivated to influence others, and some to open their mind and heart. Or perhaps these all describe one hermit over the diversity of days and years.

At an earlier time in the contemporary life of translator Red Pine, he followed his interest in these hermits to China to see if the tradition remained. He found that it did, with much retained from centuries of history and much influenced by the more recent culture and politics of China. A good friend attending a talk by Red Pine recalled him saying the contemporary hermits had health insurance and consulted ads to find a vacant cave.

I found it striking that, as Red Pine reported, the Chinese hermit tradition was not generally a life-long choice. More often, Taoists deepened their practice through several years as hermits, then returned to roles and settings with a greater degree of interaction with others. Many who lived in periods of seclusion also had periods of public service. I'm reminded of *Ten Ox Herding Pictures,* from the last of the Sung dynasty, which depicts the path of Zen, starting from the first search for tracks through the return to the world of markets and places of gathering. It seems we are describing states, not traits, when we describe ourselves as householders and as hermits.

In *Road to Heaven,* Red Pine offers a poem from 300 BCE that captures the story of Ch'u Yuan, one would-be hermit:

> when Ch'u Yuan was banished
> he wandered along rivers
> he sang on their banks
> weak and forlorn
> till a fisherman asked
> aren't you the Lord of the Gorges
> what fate has brought you to this
> and Ch'u Yuan answered
> the world is muddy
> I alone am clean

everyone is drunk
I alone am sober
and so they sent me away
and the fisherman said

a sage isn't bothered by others
he can change with the times
if the world is muddy
splash in the mire
if everyone is drunk
drink up the dregs
why get banished
for deep thought and purpose
and Ch'u Yuan said he had heard
when you clean your hair
you should dust off your hat
when you take a bath
you should shake out your robe
why should I let something so pure
be ruined and wronged by others
I'd rather jump into the Hsiang
and be buried in a fish's gut
than let something so white
be stained by common dirt...
the fisherman smiled and rowed away singing
when the Tsanglang is clear I wash my hat
when the Tsanglang is muddy I wash my feet
and once gone he was heard from no more

Poet and shaman Ch'u Yuan had been critical of the
ruler he served in the court of the state of Ch'u, so he left.

Before finding a hermitage, Ch'u Yuan threw himself into the Milo River and was lost.

My interest in the topic is not historical. I see it as our story when we choose a day, an hour, or a week of isolation for contemplation. It is our story too when we choose a morning in church or find awe in hiking. We all dance with seclusion and public service through our days and years. During a day of seclusion, we vow to the public service of saving all beings, breaking the distinctions between seclusion and service.

I find vitality in the exchanges of the fisherman and the court minister. Ch'u Yuan had done what he thought he could and despaired that it came to naught. A pause for contemplation may have helped him recognize that something white is white, and common dirt is pure as common dirt. How could they be wronged by anyone? He was not ready to hear the fisherman's advice about lying right down in the world of mud, here.

At this moment I am Ch'u Yuan railing at injustice—greed, hatred, and ignorance. In anger I reject the Middle Way and demand purity and principle of myself and others. Nothing else could be justified. We spend our days checking off groceries on a list, filing records for taxes, keeping up on the news, and caring for loved ones. We respond to the tears of the one right here and the many everywhere. There is no end of impurity. There is no time to purify.

I am the fisherman, unnamed and without rank. In the dance with wind and current, my hook and line find the shaded surface of the water and drift downstream without hesitation or rush. I offer the hook diligently as my part; the fish has the part of biting in its own time. I live at the pace of sun and river—there is no end of time.

Red Pine met a hermit in China who said most were there to practice, while some took care of shrines and temples to receive their bowl of rice. We all have our pursuits in hope of having a bowl of rice and cover from the rain. And we sit with contemplatives everywhere when taking a quiet moment in a place of practice and on a bus to work.

In his practice instructions, as translated in *Cultivating the Empty Field,* Master Hongzhi advises us in this way:

> Contemplating your own authentic form is how to contemplate Buddha. If you can experience yourself without distractions, simply surpass partiality and go beyond conceptualizing. All buddhas and all minds reach the essential without duality.

Who are you before conceptualization? Who are you before householder and hermit, competent and incompetent, confident and insecure? Meet me here and we can see, you and me. Of one thing I'm sure: We are here in the mud and the mire with a lot of company.

Of the hermits that Red Pine met, some cried tears of loneliness; some expressed contentment, volunteering that they were not lonely because of having a companion. Many worked all day in gardens for food and for something to sell in town for occasional needs. I'm reading words of another about times recent and far away, but it seems to me that as hermit and householder we are of one species.

Outside of categories, we can tend a garden to receive a bowl of rice at day's end. To do so may take a kind of discipline of body and mind, persisting in a task hour after hour. And we can fully engage with one weed, that one weed outside of time and without goal. Holding the focus is not automatic and takes its own attention. Perhaps we can call it discipline.

Whether millennia ago or in present time, these stories bring life to dedicated people of the Way—monk, nun, sadhu, or householder. All these stories include the rubbing of person against person. The vow to save all beings places us squarely in this realm of differences and strife. Purity is no salvation; not for long.

In my old field of auto safety, we worked diligently, daily, to understand the causes of vehicle injuries and fatalities and how to reduce them. Over decades, vehicles and roadways have become substantially safer. Fatalities per miles travelled in 2020 dropped to less than a third of what they were in 1965. We also knew the only way to avoid all injuries and fatalities is to have no vehicles. This tradeoff can be a community decision, and it can be a personal one we each make today in this real world of transit.

We can and should do all we can to reform police departments, even as we recognize the only way to have no police brutality is to have no police, with the possibility of trading abuse by police for crime.

Purity is a complaint against the Tao. It is like arguing with the sea for sending the wave that capsizes my boat, saying the world as it is right now should be different already. Living in the Tao is operating my boat on this sea, as it is.

Someone I know described reluctantly finding wisdom from the loss of the love of her life and again finding wisdom through her fear of a neighbor's yelling and threatening.

What she said was very close to a portion of the Greek play *Agamemnon,* written by Aeschylus in 458 BCE. Robert Kennedy extemporaneously used one translation when speaking on the day Martin Luther King died. Here is another translation:

> In visions of the night, like dropping rain,
> Descend the many memories of pain
> Before the spirit's sight: through tears and dole
> Comes wisdom o'er the unwilling soul
> A boon, I wot [know], of all Divinity,
> That holds its sacred throne in strength, above the sky!

Aeschylus writing in this poem and the woman who lost a loved one each took wisdom from riding the waves of the sea just as it is.

Our tradition leaves nothing out and directs us back to the simple and the present. In Chapter 3, "Contemplation and engagement are not separate," I included an introductory paragraph about the moment before Buddha began the exchange with Subhuti that becomes the rest of the sutra:

> One day before noon, the Bhagavan put on his patched robe, picked up his bowl, and entered the capital of Śravasti for offerings. After begging for food in the city and eating his meal of rice, he returned from his daily round in the afternoon, put his robe and bowl away,

washed his feet, and sat down on his appointed seat. After crossing his legs and adjusting his body, he turned his awareness to what was before him.

In the practice of the Middle Way, there is no error when taking care of the practical aspects of life. What do you think was the state of mind of the Buddha in the routine outlined above? What is possible for you and me in our routines today?

We can recognize the practice beyond conceptualization when there is no time and there are no categories, even as a pulled weed flops into a bucket and eyes look to the clouds as your stiff body rises and straightens. The weeds don't offer comment, perhaps making it a little easier to reach for the next without a need to justify the action. We are participants in the change of light and shadow with the sun moving east to west.

The fisherman's reply to Ch'u Yuan takes us from the garden back to the marketplace as well:

> and the fisherman said a sage isn't bothered by others
> he can change with the times
> if the world is muddy
> splash in the mire
> if everyone is drunk
> drink up the dregs
> why get banished
> for deep thought and purpose

If we take this literally, it's at best confusing; I don't know anyone who isn't bothered by others. But there is something very appealing about this poem anyway. I'm reminded of Yün-men's extending his leg as Muzhou closed a door, and

Yün-men shouting in pain when his leg was struck. Somewhere in the unambiguous explosion of pain and unimpeded scream, Yün-men's conceptions fell away. Screaming too is changing with the times and finding oneself nowhere but here, in the mud.

There are people I love and respect who see violence and abuse when, by reading of it, they splash in the mire of Yünmen's story. I know others who see stories like this as mythic or distinct from and unrelated to the anger and intentional harm of the childhood abuse they suffered. Whether you perceive these waters as clear or murky, how do you meet the world of clear and murky waters now?

We don't live in Han or Tang dynasty China, yet the hermits, current and ancestral, remind us how we can live our lives now, fully engaging. Whether working in a home garden, on a corporation-operated farm, or on a hermit's plot of land, there is one way. Whether we manage others or work alone, there is one way.

How contrasting are the perspectives of the fisherman and disgraced minister Ch'u Yuan! Ch'u Yuan said:

> I alone am clean
> everyone is drunk
> I alone am sober

The unnamed fisherman, speaking without any recognized credentials, said:

> if the world is muddy
> splash in the mire
> if everyone is drunk

drink up the dregs
why get banished

It's not difficult to understand how Ch'u Yuan could feel as he did—he was just rejected by the world he knew. Of course it's difficult to set that aside and recognize who he is. I'd be bereft and angry, I'm sure. He can't find his place anywhere, not in himself, not with others. How sad that Ch'u Yuan was not able to slow down for a time, to let the fisherman's message sink in. The fisherman was not separate from mud, drunks, or anyone else.

We also know the urge to withdraw. Even if not throwing ourselves in a river, we are disappointed by each other and evade our own thoughts by watching YouTube, eating, or writing Zen talks. When sitting silently together in a day of zazen, a wandering mind is recognizable. Whether chatting over lunch or on hold with customer service, it is also possible to "experience yourself without distraction."

We engage in zazen—listening, bowing, walking, and breathing—sometimes encouraged by feeling bothered and wanting something pure, and sometimes feeling drawn to something beyond either bothered or pure. Quoting Master Hongzhi again:

> If you can experience yourself without distractions, simply surpass partiality and go beyond conceptualizing. All buddhas and all minds reach the essential without duality.

In the quiet of our zazen, you know what to do. In the slow walk of walking meditation (kinhin), you know what to do. Carry it with you when you rise, through lunch, and running errands.

In homage to the Sabbath as an essential complement to lives of building and doing, Jewish theologian Abraham Joshua Heschel wrote:

> There is a realm of time where the goal is not to have but to be, not to own but to give, not to control but to share, not to subdue but to be in accord.

When walking with Martin Luther King, Heschel wrote that when "...I marched in Selma my feet were praying." In his recollection, Heschel is expressing something of his experience in Selma not captured by descriptions. Duality breaks down when prayer is offered by feet rather than words and lips. Distinctions of householder and hermit lose meaning if contemplation and protest entwine. We can't avoid or deny the purity within the mud of our daily lives nor the mire within the purity of days of retreat. Nor can we deny there are differences among our activities in family, work, play, and contemplation. All are essential, all are of one cloth. All can be met without conceptualization.

5
Practicing together with suffering

The cold kills you

There are koans and stories related to a driving aspect of our lives that is also at the heart of the Buddha's story. When Buddha truly recognized suffering, he left home to explore how he could live in this world of old age, sickness, and death. I find that suffering, and how we hold it, is also central to our interactions with each other. With that context, I offer this koan, from a story about Tung Shan (the teacher also known as Dongshan Liangjie), translated as Case 43 in *The Blue Cliff Record:*

> A monk asked Tung Shan, "When cold and heat come, how can we avoid them?"
>
> [Tung] Shan said, "Why don't you go to the place where there is no cold or heat?"
>
> The monk said, "What is the place where there is no cold or heat?"
>
> Tung Shan said, "When it's cold, the cold kills you; when it's hot, the heat kills you."

I've also seen the translations as "When it's cold, shiver!
When it's hot, sweat!" and "Let it kill you with the cold. Let
it kill you with the heat."

The imagery of this koan has always been striking to me.
It presents the simplicity of completely experiencing the immediate without struggle, doubt, or hesitation, leaving no room
for self or other when immersed in the experience. When tired,
yawn. When anxious, agitate. When in pain...*owww!* Within
the plain words, there is room for pain and freedom to rest
together. Right here is the fullness of experience that can
include preference, discomfort, and pain. If the facts of the
circumstances are clear and undeniable, then what more is
there to do? There are other stories which I associated with
Tung Shan's no cold or heat, such as this one:

> A woman stumbles off a cliff, and midway down she
> catches a branch and stops the fall. Looking up she sees
> there is no way to scale the shear face back to the top.
> Looking down, the climb is also impossible. There is
> no one around to help, and life is surely lost. She then
> notices beautiful berries on the end of the branch, and
> oh...they are sweet!

In a similar manner, the challenge is laid down: Release the
struggle even now, even in this desperate circumstance. If the
woman holding the branch can do it, so can I also appreciate
something of beauty, or even ugliness, now.

Using both these stories as myths, I've shared them with
cancer and chronic-pain patients. One who was subjected to
both of these scourges told me months after I shared the sheer-

cliff story that she woke up in pain every morning, at first too weak and hopeless to rise out of bed and face the day. But then she thought, "No, I've got to get up and find those berries," and so she did.

I am honored in my work to hear poignant stories of open-hearted people in searing circumstances. The stories are so tender and personal, it seemed intrusive to even ask if I could use them in a book such as this. Still, I want to speak directly to the deeply personal experience that suffering is for each of us. In this chapter I will incorporate more of my own experiences than I usually do. My hope is not to distract you with my story, but to invite you too to explore how the clenching and many-faceted ways we can suffer affect you and your relationships. How do you practice when in this bed of hot coals?

Tung Shan said, "When it's cold, the cold kills you; when it's hot, the heat kills you."

Some years ago my father died, leaving my Alzheimer's-beset mother to grieve the loss of her partner of sixty-two years. Because of her dementia, each night she forgot he died, only to wake each morning and grieve anew when she found him missing. She carried not only the sharp pain of the loss, but also shame and guilt that she could forget my father in that way. This continued for months.

In one example of her experience, a month after my father died, my mother's caregiver called me from across the country. She told me that for hours my mother had been kicking the door of the apartment in which she was locked, and my mother screamed so loudly that the other tenants were gathering, disturbed. I called my mother, who told me that she was so miserable—with nothing to live for, no future, no purpose, no activity that she could do—that she just wanted to kill herself. My mother's plan was to be horrible to be around such that others would leave her alone and let her die.

My mother's agony was real, even if her plan was distorted by her cognitive deficits. Though there was nothing of comfort I could say, she was calmer after we took time together. My mother suffered through many similar events. Each time I talked to her, my heart was broken again. Together we weep. Together we practice forbearance, the Third Paramita in Mahayana Buddhism.

Now I could stop there and say, when weeping, the weeping kills me. Perhaps it's true, and I don't doubt that the koan addresses even those moments. But in the quiet of my zazen, it did not seem enough for me at those times. I thought again about the mythic story of Buddha, who started his path upon realizing the depth of suffering in old age, sickness, and death. It was his compassion for this suffering that led him to seek and led him to the Four Noble Truths to address suffering.

In being with my mother, I could feel my own fear constrict my heart. I could not count on my mind or my practice to remember any stories or perspectives that would protect me if I suffered as she did. Whereas not long before I could suffer and be open, now I knew I was shrinking back from life, even as I recognized that my mother calmed when we were present together.

As I mentioned in relation to a different translation used in a previous chapter, Senator Robert F. Kennedy quoted Aeschylus as saying:

...Pain...falls drop by drop upon the heart until,
in our own despair, against our will,
comes wisdom...

In applying this to my mother's circumstances, I thought, "My mother has dementia and will not remember; there is no wisdom to gain, only abject suffering." Not that Aeschylus's words were wrong, but now they seemed incomplete. The Greeks, however, really knew their tragedy.

In a Greek myth, Prometheus so loved humanity that he stole fire from Zeus to bring it down to us. Zeus, not pleased, chained the immortal Prometheus to a rock. An eagle ate his liver out every day, and every night it grew back. The sentence was endless, or so it would have seemed to Prometheus, and it seems for too many of us here and now. There was no redemption, no wisdom, and nothing to attain. This story, then, touched on the reality of my mother's experience.

At an earlier time in my life, the Hebrew Bible story of Job had been my koan. The Book of Job begins with God and Satan having a conversation in which God asks Satan to appreciate the righteousness of Job; Satan tells God that Job is righteous only because God has allowed him abundance. God agrees, step by step, to allow Satan to test Job by destroying crops, killing herds, burning down structures, killing family members, and then finally subjecting Job's body to painful illnesses. Job repeatedly questions God before finally receiving an answer. Here is an example of Job's pleading and God's eventual response:

> 3:20 Wherefore is light given to him that is in misery, and life unto the bitter in soul—
> Who long for death, but it cometh not; and dig for it more than for hid treasures;
> Who rejoice unto exultation, and are glad, when they can find the grave?...
> For the thing which I did fear is come upon me, and that which I was afraid of hath overtaken me...
>
> 38:11 Then the LORD answered Job out of the whirlwind, and said:
> Who is this that darkeneth counsel by words without knowledge?...
> Where wast thou when I laid the foundations of the earth? Declare, if thou hast the understanding.
> 5 Who determined the measures thereof, if thou knowest? Or who stretched the line upon it?
> 6 Whereupon were the foundations thereof fastened? Or who laid the corner-stone thereof...
>
> 42:1 Then Job answered the LORD, and said:
> I know that Thou canst do everything, and that no purpose can be withholden from Thee...
> Therefore have I uttered that which I understood not, things too wonderful for me, which I knew not...
> I had heard of Thee by the hearing of the ear; but now mine eye seeth Thee;
> Wherefore I abhor my words, and repent, seeing I am dust and ashes.

Though I didn't interpret the Bible or the existence of God literally, at one time of my life I found this story both compelling and troubling. God's actions seemed reprehensible, and Job's response in bowing to them to be unfathomable. However, eventually, without reason and over the years, I had found comfort in the story of Job; perhaps I tired of fighting against the fact of the injustice and meaningless tragedy in the world. I could see Job as demonstrating a way to be at peace by bowing to what is and cannot be changed in the ways I'd wished, however painful.

After talking to my mother day after day, I wondered again about the story. My mother's wish for death was an echo of Job's words: "Who long for death, but it cometh not; and dig for it more than for hid treasures." What if Job didn't feel free at the end? He might have bowed and said, "I am dust and ashes," releasing any expectation that he understand, yet still unsatisfied.

I saw two possible interpretations. For one, perhaps Job's experience, or yours and mine, could be as I had previously held it: Job released struggle and bowed with acceptance. Alternatively, perhaps he bowed to the immovable force that held him, and relinquished expectation that he should or even could understand, and still churned at the injustice and all the losses. Each of these is a description of how we meet the world. Each can be the way in a given moment in which we relinquish ourselves to the world we meet.

With similar ambiguity, the poet Bashō wrote:

soon to die
yet showing no sign
in the cicada's voice

Perhaps the cicada chirps for the sake of it, showing us a way to live in a world of danger without inhibiting fear. Or perhaps it is screaming. In yet another example, Mark reported the final words of Jesus:

My God, why hast thou forsaken me?

These words express inescapable suffering, without reservation or mediation. They demonstrate that as mature a figure as Jesus was portrayed to be, his humanity could not be suppressed. Such emotional charge is often fully expressed in the stories of Western heritage. The East had and has its way as well.

Within the commentary associated with Case 46 of *The Blue Cliff Record* is this exchange:

Ch'ing asked, "What is the sound outside the gate?"

A monk said, "The sound of a snake eating a frog."

Ch'ing said, "I knew that sentient beings suffer: here is another suffering sentient being."

In these decades or centuries of translation of the ancient way of the Buddha to our Western culture, we all find our means to make the Buddha Way our own.

I have always loved the sparse aesthetic of China and Japan, but in the time after my father died, the direct and passionate images of Western traditions resonated more deeply. However, such differences show up among Western traditions as well.

A wonderful woman I knew talked about the need to some-
times access the beatific Christ images of the Eastern Orthodox
Church and at other times the gory Christ images of Central
American Catholicism.

In chanting the Heart Sutra at Three Treasures Sangha,
we say:

> ...in emptiness there is...no suffering, cause of
> suffering, cessation, path...

In the way I've presented the stories of my mother, Job,
Jesus, and one perspective on the cicada, we could think of
them as representing the "no cessation" aspect of this sutra.
Speaking personally, I do find freedom in the more inclusive
and unmitigated suffering in some of these stories. I don't
think I'm overreaching to say that even with the best practice,
we can't always cease suffering in the ways we wish. Still, all
these stories can carry the spirit of Tung Shan's "the heat kills
you" and the Heart Sutra's "no suffering."

Job sincerely appealed to God, without damning, crying
again and again, "Why?" Is that not his investigation of the
Great Matter in the face of the suffering in this life? I see this
as Job's "leaving home" in the way Buddha left home in the
face of suffering. Job's entreaties were not wasted. In the story,
God in his own time replied, "Who is this that darkeneth
counsel by words without knowledge?" Perhaps in the cultural language of Jews of old, God's response offered the same
pointer as Bodhidharma in ancient China, answering "I don't
know" when asked who he was. Job could not know why.
Perhaps Job, in his cultural language, expressed his humanity

and acceptance of the mystery of that which is beyond words by referring to himself as "dust and ashes."

Prometheus's story didn't end in chains. An unknown time later, Hercules shot the eagle with an arrow and Prometheus's chains were broken. Yet until the day Hercules arrived, Prometheus was in pain "forever." Just as in Tung Shan's "The heat kills you," the beak of the eagle in his flesh was all Prometheus knew on the rock.

On the cross, Jesus quoted the first line of Psalm 22 of David in asking why God had forsaken him; Jesus's experience was different three days later. David's well-known Psalm 23 begins "The Lord is my shepherd, I shall not want," again pointing to the impermanence of both being forsaken and being saved. Can you say which of being forsaken and being saved is letting the heat kill you, and which is letting the cold kill you?

Although Tung Shan's teaching could be absolutely right in its content, in terms of the impact of the imagery, sometimes I personally miss the grittiness of the culture of my Detroit upbringing. Your experience need not be the same, as you find your way to receive the ancient stories and words and meld them into your life here and now. Still, with images of the sharpness of the eagle's beak and the boils on Job's skin, we know that we're talking about the passionate depth of human experience. By linking Tung Shan's hot and cold with these familiar stories of Western tradition, we can more easily live in both the inescapable suffering and our human limitations in avoiding it.

The humanity of our suffering and the limitations in avoiding it link us together, ancient and current. In our pain we can cause pain in those around us. The pain of those around us can lead to our pain. When intolerable, we can seek solutions that cause more pain. In his memoir, Danny Trejo— addict, violent convict, and later, drug counselor and Hollywood actor—wrote about the moment after injecting heroin:

> Bam. When it hit me, the boogeyman was gone. The boogeyman was that feeling of regret about the past and fear about the future. Like a lot of addicts, I was full of myself while at the same time exploding with self-hatred. I'd feel remorse, then fear, then anger in that order and sometimes I'd move through the first two in less than a second. My anger turned outward, to blame. I would blame outside people, places, and things for the fucked-up state I found myself in, never once taking a hard look at myself and taking responsibility for the situation I was in. All of these conflicting feelings would overwhelm me and that's where heroin stepped in. Heroin was my escape hatch. It had been ever since I first used it, at twelve, to avoid the anger in my house.

Trejo later tells of being in Soledad prison, waiting to be charged with capital crimes for throwing a rock at the head of a guard in prison. When he faced the death penalty, fear brought him back to the faith of his youth, which killed the old gangster-Trejo. He left the home of his old ways.

For each of us, inescapable suffering is a call to leave home—to leave the familiar ways we think, respond, and demand of ourselves and others around us. When the eagle ate his liver, Prometheus might not have noticed whether sweet berries were nearby. "The heat kills you." To demand he see the berries or to demand my mother accept my father's death might make you or me feel better by creating a separation between them and us, or by imagining we or anyone could do otherwise. With "the cold kills you," Tung Shan points another way.

It seems that, again and again, part of practice is composed of abandoning the very words used to describe practice itself— practice becoming a barrier to practice. The call to take refuge continually arises anew, pointing to the utterly human experience beyond words such as *refuge, suffering, no-self,* and *practice.* Killed by heat, killed by cold; in the wordless silence, all is well.

I find no words sufficient to express the role of practicing alone and together in the face of suffering. But I bow to the altar, to you, and the cushions, and sit right here. Together we sit, sinking in, breathing, screaming with our own loved ones, weeping with the families of shooting victims, feeling resentful and terrified with those fearing the loss of ability to support family.

When cringing, the cringing kills you. When open, the openness kills you. We share this ground with all beings.

6

Loneliness without separation

Bare mountains and fallen leaves

We are social creatures all. Shame and embarrassment are
intense emotions arising from our awareness of others, the
need to belong, to be respected, and to be cared for. Loneliness
is compelling as a special case of suffering. Ryōkan Taigu, the
nineteenth-century Zen Buddhist monk who lived much of
his life as a hermit, wrote the following poem, as translated by
John Stevens in *One Robe, One Bowl:*

> Loneliness
> In the blue sky a winter goose cries.
> The mountains are bare; nothing but falling leaves.
> Twilight: returning along the lonely village path
> Alone, carrying an empty bowl.
> Foolish and stubborn—what day can I rest?
> Lonely and poor, this life.
> Twilight: I return from the village
> Again carrying an empty bowl.

My urge to share small observations and experiences was
one of the most striking and memorable aspects that arose

from the silence of my first sesshin. I didn't know the norms nor anyone there, so even nonverbal communication was missing. Without the silence, I would not have known how many times a day I sought the touchstone of shared reality. In the first days, I'd observe or experience something, and the thought would arise, "I've gotta remember this to tell..." without necessarily knowing who I would tell it to. By the end of the first day it was clear that I would not remember what I wanted to say anyway.

I was equally struck by the same need to connect when I was single and living in a four-plex with dear friends. Most days after work we shared just a few brief words. I was again shocked by the enormous difference it made to do so

We are also living through an epidemic of loneliness that began even before the forced isolation of the Covid pandemic. The results of a Cigna and Ipsos survey showed that 40 percent of adults eighteen and older felt alone, and 43 percent reported that they lacked meaningful relationships and felt left out. A summary statement in the study concluded this:

> In all the findings, a lack of meaningful human connectedness is paramount.

In our culture of independence, I see people doubting themselves when lonely, as if self-sufficiency should eliminate loneliness. Foxes tend to hunt, travel, and live alone, while wolves live together in packs without being subject to our criticism. Why doubt or shame ourselves when we long to be in a tribe?

Looking at Ryōkan's poem in the opening to this chapter, we can see that it's not *just* about loneliness.

Returning home in the evening light carrying an empty bowl can express loneliness, but without contradiction it can also represent non-separation from the cry of a goose and nothing but falling leaves on bare mountains.

This poem by Chao-chou, from Tang dynasty China and translated in *The Recorded Sayings of Zen Master Joshu,* shows there is nothing new about loneliness and non-separation:

> Sun level with the ground. The second hour of the day.
>
> A broken down temple in a deserted village—there's nothing worth saying about it.
>
> In the morning gruel there's not a grain of rice,
>
> Idly facing the open window and its dirty cracks.
>
> Only the sparrows chattering, no one to be friends with,
>
> Sitting alone, now and then hearing fallen leaves hurry by.
>
> Who said that to leave home is to cut off likes and dislikes?
>
> If I think about it, before I know it there are tears moistening my hanky.

Chao-chou (also known as Joshu in Japanese) lived to be 120 years old (778–897). Chao-chou and Ryōkan are both respected ancestors in our Zen tradition. The writings left by both of them undeniably reveal that each at times experienced feeling bereft and lonely. It seems that years of dedicated Zen training does not guarantee we will avoid the bone-chill of loneliness. How are we to understand this? Does it raise doubt about the potential this practice offers you and me?

There is relevance here of Tung Shan saying, "When it's cold, the cold kills you." But let's not dismiss our doubt by referencing a koan, and instead honor the question. The question, too, is human, and it was stated in the words of the Buddha, recorded in the Sallattha Sutra this way:

> Monks, an uninstructed run-of-the-mill person feels feelings of pleasure, feelings of pain, feelings of neither-pleasure-nor-pain. A well-instructed disciple of the noble ones also feels feelings of pleasure, feelings of pain, feelings of neither-pleasure-nor-pain. So what difference, what distinction, what distinguishing factor is there between the well-instructed disciple of the noble ones and the uninstructed run-of-the-mill person?

That question from the first century BCE is so close to ours that it needs no comment or clarification. Buddha went on to explain:

> So...[the uninstructed run-of-the-mill person] feels two pains, physical and mental. Just as if they were to shoot a man with an arrow and, right afterward, were to shoot him with another one, so that he would feel the pains of two arrows, in the same way. When touched with a feeling of pain, the uninstructed run-of-the-mill person sorrows, grieves, and laments, beats his breast, becomes distraught. So he feels two pains, physical and mental.

The Pali word used in the sutra that was translated as *mental* is also shown in a Pali dictionary as meaning *mind, consciousness,* and *thought.* The early Buddhists created overlapping, multi-layered, and nuanced lists of mind states within *consciousness.* One list of fifty-two mind states was broken down into categories of states, including universal, occasional, unwholesome, and beautiful. To give an idea of this list, the universal category has seven states, including sensations, feelings, perceptions, and attention. The unwholesome category has fourteen states, including shamelessness, hatred, and skeptical doubt.

Buddha reminded us that when shot by an arrow we cannot escape the direct experience of it—*Arghh!* The second arrow contains other experiences, such as the need to deny and escape. Running will not help; the arrow will come with us. The second arrow carries the concepts that explain the feelings and also that blind us to truth outside our explanations.

All fifty-two mind states are described as conditioned and impermanent. All are carried by the second arrow.

Loneliness is a feeling we know, and it's a word that is not the feeling. The word does not, cannot, capture our own unique and pervasive loneliness in a given moment. As Zen adepts, the seeming contradiction between loneliness and non-separation is particularly helpful in that it highlights the limits of conceptualization. We don't have any trouble seeing how at the same time I can be hungry, have an aching toe, and miss my deceased father. That same moment can include the fallen leaves on a bare mountain and much more. Why not recognize loneliness and non-separation, fallen leaves, and much more?

Releasing concepts to recognize much more is zazen.

Recognizing much more is to avoid the restrictions of what zazen is, who I am, who you are, and lonely and not lonely. Zazen is not protective; it is a release to a state of greater simplicity. Can you meet loneliness with utter simplicity?

I've known people who fear the medication that reduces their hallucinations of others interacting with them because they don't want to lose the relationships. This is not so different from any of us staying in an unsatisfying relationship because of the fear of being alone if we leave it. Closer to our daily experiences, we've all been the person standing on the sidelines in a group, feeling unlike others and alone. It's hard to engage without a point of commonality, and it's hard to leave when we want to belong.

How much of the tension and divisiveness in the world around us is the heat generated from our differences and disagreements? I don't mean to imply an answer by raising the question—I don't know. But it seems human history has always been tribal. In the shadow side of the tribal, I'm sure my view is correct, my solution the best, if only you'd agree and comply. There's nothing evil implied here, just fear, pain, and protectiveness of ourselves and the ones we love.

We have imminent and global threats of climate change, pandemics, and the unregulated emergence of artificial intelligence. We may not even agree on what to add to the list of dangers. To address such questions, no matter the list, we need cooperation. Part of that cooperation is to meet each other with open hearts even when we vehemently disagree. We saw with the Covid response in the U.S. that we enacted no one's ideal solution and still saved millions of lives.

Chao-Chou had his way, rising for another day. The ripples of his presence have circled the world without ceasing. Ryōkan had his way, wandering the country and writing poems so that we could recognize the bare mountains and falling leaves here. We each have our way when sitting on black cushions and bowing at the sound of the bell. And we each have our way when leaving the dojo and returning to the marketplace. There are no contradictions among these—not when we sit quietly, and not when we rise and speak.

Living into loneliness is like hiking in the rain. There can be freedom in the warm sun; under a raincoat there may be a constrained quality instead. With one's head covered by a rain hood, the sounds of some birds are inaudible and those that remain are muffled. While cautious of where to sit, there are no panoramic views; we walk cloaked, in our own world. On such a day, the relative freedom of sun does not exist, and it's as if it never has and never will.

Living into such a day can also be rich with the syncopated rhythm of droplets on our hood and jewel-like beads of water on pine needles that dive to earth when ready. The thirst of all beings is quenched by rivulets of muddy water underfoot, lit without shadow under a clouded sky. This is the hike of the instructed one to whom Buddha referred.

Living into loneliness—into any mood—can be like this too. One day in this world as it is can be infused by longing. Loneliness can be sharpest when we share a home with the one we love but from whom, for this moment, we are estranged by tension over something that means nothing to either of us. Loneliness gives a noir cast to the sound of the furnace kicking in and the slow gurgling of the coffee pot. One life as it is.

It can be easier (on a good day) sitting on our cushions to take a breath as it is, light patterns on the floor as they are, without thought of breath, one breathing, or light. Carrying that to standing and walking without concept of standing and walking, the unidentifiable distinction is made between the uninstructed and the instructed. Note that in the Sallattha Sutra, Buddha didn't offer instruction, only that there is a difference when releasing the second arrow that carries the skandhas of concepts.

Contrast is low under the clouded sky. Distinctions made to clarify a mood can offer something when used moderately. Distinctions—*why...if only...next time...*—can also obscure the simplicity of the rhythm of the rain and a sigh of loneliness.

We have a warm response in seeing a familiar view of a prominent feature—a tree, a mountain, a friend's house. On a foggy day when the feature is hidden, we have another response; we see what we see and can't help but also register that which we don't see. The tree or mountain are prominent in their presence and also in their absence. The presence and absence of a lost loved one in our home similarly registers. Our bodies respond differently when recognizing presence and when recognizing absence, and at the same time, presence and absence are inextricably linked, not two.

There is no protection when we live into even this—
grief, loneliness, shame, love—and there is no exhausting
struggle when we release impotent attempts to protect. A sigh
remains. This doesn't make anything better, but it helps dissolve
the villains and heroes from the story.

In a poem in *Crow with no Mouth*, the soulful fifteenth-
century Japanese teacher Ikkyū writes:

> my friend's funeral this morning
> burns inside me like my own death

And he wrote this one:

> I was like an old leafless tree until we met green buds
>   burst and blossom
> now that I have you I'll never forget what I owe you

Loneliness and connectedness are the warp and weft of
one fabric. Joy and sorrow are also woven in, each with moist
tears. To have something and to not have something circle
the same mandala; no separation.

Find the view from a position off the mind road. Mind
wants to describe by lining up words one at a time in sentences
with rules of grammar. Off the mind road, there is a splash of
simultaneous and direct experience: Love and loss; excitement
for and relief to not have to. When words are quiet and all
things are empty, the world is full and all in it dances. And
yet, in that same moment, I am in the chorus of those bereft
and without companionship, including Bashō when he wrote
this haiku:

turn this way!
I too feel lonely
late in autumn

I'll end with a verse from one of the sutras that describes the intimacy coincident in the world of distinctions, articulated even in its title, The Tallying of Difference and Sameness:

In the very midst of light, there's darkness,
but don't take darkness as its equivalent.
In the very midst of darkness, there's light,
but don't take light as enhancing vision.
Light and dark respond to one another,
cooperating like front and back legs, walking.

7

The practice of mutual support

Linji asks for instruction

There is so much in the following story from *The Record of Linji*. Its plot tells how an influential teacher began on the path and later will come to recognize what was always there:

> When Linji was one of the assembly of monks under Huangbo, he was plain and direct in his behavior. The head monk praised him saying: "Though he's a youngster, he is different from the other monks." So he asked: "Honorable monk, how long have you been here?"
>
> "Three years," replied Linji.
>
> "Have you ever asked for instruction?"
>
> "No, I've never asked for instruction. I don't know what to ask," replied Linji.
>
> "Why don't you go ask the head priest of this temple just what the cardinal principle of the Buddhadharma is?" said the head monk.
>
> Linji went and asked. Before he had finished speaking, Huangbo hit him. Linji came back. "How did your question go?" asked the head monk.

"Before I had finished speaking the Master hit me. I don't understand," said Linji.

"Then go and ask him again," said the head monk.

So Linji went back and asked, and again Huangbo hit him. Thus Linji asked the same question three times and was hit three times.

While our practice seems—and in ways is—solitary, this story also demonstrates that we are mutually engaged in practice in critical and meaningful ways. In this chapter, we cultivate the ground of mutual support as presented in our tradition and as we can make it our own in our daily lives.

The recorded story of Linji did not include much about his early practice. It begins when the head monk notices that Linji is plain and direct. That Linji described his own early practice as "exhaustive investigation" adds to the story. He is supported by the unnamed head monk and the teachers Huangbo and Dayu, and also by his own intention and practice. As the story begins, Linji is supported first by being seen: The head monk notices Linji and acts on what he sees.

We can take a different perspective in our description of these events as well. Perhaps the head monk found ease and support from the plain and direct manner of this young man, and thus took notice. The interaction cannot be separated as to who supported whom, who initiated, who is teacher, and who is student.

In *Encouraging Words,* Robert Aitken wrote:

Zazen is not a practice of isolation. It is not a sensory deprivation chamber. Speculation, planning, remembering, fantasizing—these are things that deprive you as you sit there on your cushions.

We celebrate the great enlightenment of the Buddha Shākyamuni in this sesshin and realize that all beings are the Tathāgatha and depend upon each other. This is called mutual interdependence or dependent arising; for our purposes it means that each of us is a teacher supporting everyone else, and each of us is a student, being supported by everyone else. Let's celebrate in this spirit.

So our story moves with mutual support evident in the interactions between the actors exhibiting a diversity of support. The head monk's kind and affirming encouragement of Linji is similar to how we often think of the word *supportive.* Apparently, Huangbo's support was through interruption and a hit—less familiar gestures of support in our age and culture.

After Linji returned from his third meeting with Huangbo, the story continues:

> Linji came back and said to the head monk: "It was so kind of you to send me to question the Master. Three times I asked him and three times I was hit by him. I regret that some obstruction caused by my own past karma prevents me from grasping his profound meaning. I'm going away for a while."
>
> The head monk said, "If you are going away, you should go take your leave of the Master." Linji bowed low and withdrew.
>
> The head monk went to the Master's quarters before Linji, and said: "The young man who has been ques-

tioning you is a man of dharma. If he comes to take his leave, please handle him expediently. In the future, with training, he is sure to become a great tree which will provide cool shade for the people of the world."

Linji came to take his leave. Huangbo said: "You mustn't go anywhere else but to Dayu's place by the river in Gao'an. He's sure to explain things for you."

Aitken Roshi made the point that our practice is not in isolation. Linji practiced diligently in the monastery for three years, apparently without individual instruction, although in the fold of sangha. Through his personal practice he was receptive, ready for a spark. Whatever the state he achieved on the cushion, when he rose, he was open to receiving teaching and open about not even knowing what to ask. This not knowing is most intimate.

We can't know what would have happened if the head monk had restricted his own practice to sitting in the dojo, but we do know the spark came to Linji in interactions with and through the support of others. Supported by his own practice, Linji was not distracted when in the Chinese version, the head monk called him shang-tso (translated as "honorable monk") rather than by his name. Shang-tso means "lower seat," a lower rank. Linji did not get lost in this designation, accepting the role but not the implication that he was less than.

When I was at Dai Bosatsu Zendo in New York, there were many stories of Soen Roshi. In one, Soen walked through the kitchen during sesshin and asked the cook what she was doing. The cook said, "I am cooking to feed all beings." Soen nodded and walked on. The next day and the day after, Soen and the cook repeated this exchange. After the cook's response on the third day, Soen loudly slammed his open palm on the counter and said, "No! It is *your* practice!" The cook still felt Soen's support when she told me the story years later.

Soen reminded the cook that her practice was to cook. That too is the nature of our practices, yours and mine, off the cushion. The head monk at Huangbo's place wasn't doing something supportive, he was being head monk; it was his practice to engage Linji. This action from the place of no thoughts is without distinction of one doing for another, as the sun rises without a thought of warming the earth. There is no such thing as support when there is not two, and not one, and so we call it support.

I said earlier that Huangbo's support was hitting and interrupting, but that is a description of what we might see with our eyes while not seeing the nature of his support. Linji asked for the cardinal rule of the Buddhadharma; Huangbo responded directly. Any explanation would have been a deception. Huangbo's interruption of the question was an affirmative response, like attending to breath is a response to the recognition of a thought arising during zazen.

And Huangbo was not supportive; it was his practice as Ho-shang—that is, as master.

The passage in which Linji despaired of understanding stood out for me too. He told the head monk, "I'm going away for a while." The head monk said, "If you are going away, you should go take your leave of the Master." Support in this moment was in what the head monk chose not to do. He did not generate hope and did not comfort. He was in a manner respectful that Linji could handle his own discomfort and in fact was on to something. The head monk let him go. And as Soen demonstrated for the cook, just cooking was enough, was practice, and was everything necessary in that moment. No grand answers because there are no grand questions.

For Linji, the hitting and lack of reassurance were encouragement. I can't say how many other students of Huangbo went away in despair and left practice, nor do I understand the cultural differences in how Chinese adepts in the Tang dynasty may have responded. The example does raise a question about how we Americans encourage each other in the twenty-first century West. Can we exhort more and offer less understanding? Perhaps, and perhaps not. Certainly there is no answer consistent with each individual or for all circumstances.

Exhortations can stoke the fires that motivate us to taste the fruits of the Buddha Way with our own tongues. They can also bring overly stringent ideas that make the Buddha Way into an arid path traversed relentlessly, with intensity and cruel demands that lead to despair for some of us—or for all of us some of the time. Alternatively, if imbalanced in our emphasis on our being already here, whether recognized or not, do we miss the so-near oasis where we can quench our thirst for the Buddha Way? The balance of exhortation and patience is part of the translation of Zen to the West, and finding *our* way is an ongoing endeavor. This balance is also a koan of its own, addressed by each of us as we decide when to sit, when to rest, and how to apply ourselves while sitting.

This koan is yours day by day: How do you engage in practice without self-judgment and with appropriate care for your body? This is the Middle Way that the historical Buddha founded when he broke tradition and accepted milk from a woman walking to market. Whether he did so out of misery or new creativity, the milk refreshed his strength as he walked the Way. As the myth goes, when Buddha took nutrition, he lost the respect of his practice community.

The unnamed woman's practice was not to hit but to offer milk. By this simple act she played an essential part in the formation of the tradition we share today. It is likely she never knew her role. What do you think is her seat, low rank or high rank?

This old story of Linji reminds us of the complexity of finding our own way to apply ourselves to practice. And equally it highlights the complexity of encouraging the sangha members accompanying us. Don't let that stop you from offering milk to the ones you see by the side of the road who lost their strength. Support is a living koan indeed.

Returning to Linji's journey:

> Linji arrived at Dayu's temple. Dayu said: "Where have you come from?"
>
> "I have come from Huangbo's place," replied Linji.
>
> "What did Huangbo have to say?" asked Dayu.

"Three times I asked him just what the cardinal principle of the Buddhadharma was and three times he hit me. I don't know whether I was at fault or not."

"Huangbo is such a grandmother that he utterly exhausted himself with your troubles!" said Dayu. "And now you come here asking whether you were at fault or not!"

At these words Linji attained great enlightenment. "Ah, there isn't so much to Huangbo's Buddhadharma!" he cried.

Dayu grabbed hold of Linji and said: "You bed-wetting little devil! You just finished asking whether you were at fault or not, and now you say, "There isn't so much to Huangbo's Buddhadharma." What did you just see? Speak, speak!

Linji jabbed Dayu in the side three times.

We don't know how much time passed between Linji leaving Huangbo's place and arriving Dayu's, but Linji was active along the way. Before leaving, he talked only of his own past karmic obstructions to understanding; upon arriving, he was starting to open to another perspective and so questioned: Was I at fault or not? It seems that during his travels, he was teacher to himself, beginning to listen and receive support from himself.

Just as important as seeking help from others at times is turning to Mu, to breath, to the sound of the traffic. Turn towards this as just this, and turn again, patiently.

After arriving where Huangbo directed him, Dayu supported Linji by seemingly dismissing him. Though doubtless the straightforward Linji expressed his distress at being struck and failing to understand, Dayu again supported by pointing, though not comforting or affirming ordinary perspectives. Four times Linji asked about the cardinal principle of the Buddhadharma. We could easily imagine an adept at this point, self-doubting and tired, lying down in resignation and despair. In arriving before Dayu, Linji had done all that was asked: He did it all as instructed, and was again told he was dense and, by the way, imposing on Dayu's time as well.

Instead, Linji heard the message that was intended. No need to look to Dayu for the answer; no need to travel anywhere. Even further, Dayu might be understood as saying, "I won't burden you with an answer that will impede you with even more ideas. You already have all that you need." Why explain? The question about the cardinal principle of the Buddhadharma was like asking directions to the water while standing in the river. If I do that, please splash me!

Every koan is a demonstration of support. Many times what is offered is like Huangbo's response—apparently no answer, no guideline, and nothing left to hold on to. Or like Bodhidharma telling the emperor of China that all his good works garner no merit. Is Bodhidharma's response blunt dismissal or did it actively point to something else?

Other ancestors have their own ways of demonstration. In "Jinniu's Rice Bucket," Case 74 of *The Blue Cliff Record,* we are told:

Every day, before the midday meal, Master Jinniu himself would carry the rice tub into the monks' hall, do a dance before them, laughing loudly, and say, "Little bodhisattvas, come eat your rice!"

Xuedou said, "Although he acted like that, he was not kind-hearted."

Master Jinniu joyously, warmly, offered rice without being any more kind than a mother feeding a child or the sun warming my face. Soen would have approved of Xuedou's comment— it was Jinniu's practice!

These are all just fine stories of old if we don't make them our own by living them. My focus here is on the web of support that captures us all. How do we practice, whether in the dojo or not, as teacher supporting all, and how do we practice as students being supported by all?

There is a koan in our tradition: "How do you teach the Dharma to a baby?"

I was recently at a wonderful aquarium in Atlanta, standing before a tank of enormous seals. The crowd in which I stood could see the seals breaking the surface of the water and rolling gracefully while diving deep, circling the tank and each other, smoothly and gently brushing the walls and the glass. Within the crowd there was a child, maybe eighteen months old, on the shoulders of her father. She loudly squealed with joy at the motion of these beautiful animals, her arms irrepressibly, celebratorily, waving above her head. With each squeal, I laughed. We all laughed. The exuberant joy was contagious. There was only one joy in that crowd.

Koans of support are everywhere. Who was teaching the Dharma to whom that day?

I can't help but feel warm, even tearful in thinking about that beautiful child. There is another example that has stayed in my mind, this one more interactive. One Christmas season, my wife and I treated ourselves to a live performance of the Total Experience Gospel Choir. We were far back in a large hall. Leah LaBelle, then a very young girl, came out to sing a solo before this enormous crowd. At parts, she struggled and appeared nervous. Individuals throughout the auditorium rose independently as she sang, shouting things like, "Sing it!" and "You got it, girl!" The shouts echoed in the hall with resounding and heartfelt encouragement. For me it was the most moving moment of the evening.

For all of us in the world, we are called to a broad receptivity as well. What is it to be supportive right now? What is action in support of this one body we all share? That may be to take time alone to sit, sleep, or exercise. Or, at other times, to cook, to garden at my house or the dojo, or to help a friend clean out a house. Whatever the action, it is your practice. This practice includes first the question: What is it to be supportive right now?

Receptivity for the head monk meant noticing the cool shade already evident around Linji. Without receptivity, the head monk could instead have noticed what was missing in this quiet monk who couldn't even figure out how to ask a question. Receptivity for Linji meant his wondering what the teaching was in being hit.

What is it to be supportive right now? To open the answer is to be willing to be generous to this skin bag here and now, and willing to be generous to something not defined by the boundary skin. To truly address this question, like any koan, requires a receptiveness beyond distinctions of inside and outside. Now, what is it to be supportive? There is also no need to wait for some imagined future state of clarity to answer. There is no way to avoid responding by our action or inaction now. Anything you say or do will be the response.

As we reflect on this, I'm cautious of the language of mutual support, interdependence, and dependent arising that can sound deceptively grand, but it need not be so. The floor under our cushions and feet supports us in a tangible way. It does so whether we notice it or not.

Affliction too supports us in our practice, no less than the floor upon which we sit. It doesn't ask our gratitude for its role, which is probably a good thing. I suspect we could use that word *affliction* to describe the spark lighting Linji on his journey that led him to recognize there was not so much to Huangbo's Buddhadharma. Not so much, and yet Linji did become a tree to shade others in their own dance with affliction.

Support is as simple as offering milk to a man weak with hunger. Support is as impactful as a German family hiding Jews in Nazi Germany. Scholars after the war could not find what was different about the 0.5 percent of Germans who were willing to hide Jews and risk the brutal death of their own families. The one thing they had in common was that when asked why they agreed to this support, they said, "I had no other choice." I imagine families that did not help would also have said they had no choice but to protect their own families—a fine reminder to us all to not dismiss your contribution or diminish whatever it is you can offer. This too is the Way.

The deep challenge to this koan of support is less identifiable when we are full, when time and energy for practice and service are abundant. The challenge arises when we are depleted, ill, or hungry; that is, human. Prioritizing practice can support me, and it can support others when, by sitting, I have greater receptivity in interactions. I regularly hear from people their dilemmas about balancing practice, work, family, world affairs, and, especially, sleep. I suspect each of you experiences a version of this as well. How do you choose in this moment? Or how do you respond when you are with someone else grappling with such choices? Do you offer suggestions as the head monk did for Linji? Or respond by sweeping away the question as Huangbo did? Or warmly offer sustenance as Master Jinnui did?

Hold the question dearly—it is your koan. Act, don't act, wrestle, doubt, and foster receptivity to a response yet to be recognized. The range of responses is broad, and I fully trust in the messiness we all share in the examination. Beyond right and wrong, by responding and being open to the experience of ease and discord, we find our way.

This is a koan of a lifetime, always changing, always returning. What can we do but embrace it?

8

The koan of groups

Don't think good, don't think evil

The koan in this chapter addresses how you and I live in this world of pain and beauty. How do we navigate the circumstance in which we find ourselves? How do we join together today and recognize that place to which you or I might seek while navigating, when the choices we have are all undesirable, if not aversive to us?

In our family, work, and community lives, discernment beyond rules calls for our attention. How do we foster receptivity to the whispering place from which openness and creativity arise?

For me, returning to receptivity requires release of the ideas I start with, open to what may feel unconfined by this skin. My deepest wish is to offer no wisdom or answers but to invite you to yours.

Before I present the koan, I'll offer some background about Case 23 from the koan collection, *The Gateless Barrier,* titled "Neither good nor evil." As the story goes, Hui-neng was a poor, uneducated lay person from the south of China

who had been staying for a time at the monastery of the teacher
Hung-jen, the fifth in succession after Bodhidharma brought
Buddhism to China from India. As it happened, Hung-jen
decided he was ready to choose a successor and step down; he
asked anyone interested in taking his job to write a poem on
the monastery wall, expressing their understanding.

As translated, the poem of the head monk, Ming, is this:

> The body is the Bodhi Tree;
> the mind is like a clear mirror;
> moment by moment, wipe the mirror carefully;
> let there be no dust upon it.

Who is there to wipe the dust? We see here the clear sitting
we all know and the remaining separation. There is meditating, and there is awareness of meditating.

Expanding on one reference in the koan, when Buddha
resolved to set all other pursuits aside, he sat until he awoke
under the Bodhi Tree.

Everyone thought Ming was *the one,* and no one else offered a poem. That is, until Hui-neng came out of the kitchen
after work, saw the poem, asked someone what was going on,
and then asked to have the poem read to him. I imagine Hui-
neng saying something like, "That's not right. Can you write
one for me?" Hui-neng dictated this poem:

> Bodhi really has no tree;
> the mirror too has no stand;
> from the beginning there's nothing at all;
> where can any dust alight?

All swept away from the beginning.

When seeing the poem dictated by the illiterate Hui-neng, the old teacher called for him in private. After talking, the old teacher gave his robe and bowl to Hui-neng as a symbol of the transmission, but also advised that he flee from the jealousy of the monks. Taking it even further, that same night Hung-jen himself rowed Hui-neng across the river to help him on his way. This was wise, as the assembly of monks gave chase. The head monk, Ming, was former military, strong of body and will, and left the others behind.

As translated in *The Gateless Barrier,* here is the koan case:

> The Sixth Ancestor was pursued by Ming the head monk as far as Ta-Yu Peak. The teacher, seeing Ming coming, laid the robe and bowl on a rock and said, "This robe represents the Dharma. There should be no fighting over it. You may take it back with you."
>
> Ming tried to lift it up, but it was immovable as a mountain. Shivering and trembling, he said, "I came for the Dharma, not for the robe. I beg you, Lay brother, please open the Way for me."
>
> The teacher said, "Don't think good; don't think evil. At this very moment, what is the original face of Ming, the head monk?"
>
> In that instant Ming had great satori. Sweat ran from his entire body. In tears he made his bows saying, "Beside these secret words and secret meanings, is there anything of further significance?"
>
> The teacher said, "What I have just conveyed is not secret. If you reflect on your own face, whatever is secret will be right there with you."

Over years, I savored this koan for the rich perspectives of Hui-neng (the one in the story who was given the robe and bowl, then ran), and Ming (the head monk who chased him). The story also offers the opportunity for reflection about the perspective of the community. In the story of Hui-neng, the community has an active role, and it isn't a flattering one. Reading it, including the description of their jealousy and knowing that Hui-neng became the sixth patriarch, we also know that the community is on the losing side of history. It is natural to be dismissive of their participation in the story. I ask that we together step back from that conclusion and instead join the assembly ourselves. Doing so, we now both join in the koan and bring it to life as we will experience it today and tomorrow in our own lives.

Bear with me while I indulge in making up a scene for the assembly back then, which might be closer to the difficulty in discernment that we encounter today. Perhaps the community then had been aware of the decline of their teacher, old man Hung-jen, who was forgetting things, making mistakes, and less aware of the everyday activities of the monastery.

Perhaps also the community had been grateful for the steady guidance and competence of the head monk, Ming, in maintaining and inspiring practice and practical function.

Further, perhaps they didn't know Hui-neng except for his odd, illiterate, south-China behaviors. Individuals in the community would then likely have a lot of reasonable fears and questions, which might be like these:

Even if Hui-neng wrote a lovely poem, how can we trust turning our lives and futures over to this character? Will he be able to interact with the wider community to assure the donations we need to survive? Is the old man really losing it and unable to understand the choice he's making? One poem can't possibly be enough to make the important decision the old man just made. We clearly know head monk Ming better than the old man does. I love this practice and monastery; I owe Huang-mei temple my very life. In gratitude and reverence, I must respond to preserve the Dharma assets for others as well as myself.

If something like this were the experience and understanding of you or me, we might well give chase to seek the return of the bowl and robe. I might well do so to correct the injustice of the choice with respect to Ming and to alleviate the suffering that will arise by the squandering of the Dharma assets of the monastery:

> Just as one might feel compelled to join an anti-abortion movement to alleviate the suffering of unborn children and uphold the principle (justice) of not killing.
>
> Just as one might feel compelled by the principle (justice) to join a movement to support the right to choose abortion to alleviate the suffering of unwanted children, of women who might otherwise get illegal abortions, and of choice over one's own body and belief.
>
> Just as one might speak passionately for each side of any choice that is as important to others as it is to you, yet others' approaches are anathema to you.

In such moments—my way or your way—our understanding may be right or it may be mistaken. Yet we cannot escape the call for a response; it's up to us to find a fitting response. What is your way of recognizing *your* response in these moments of the deepest disagreements about issues of grave importance?

Returning to the story, in the moment of any vehement or modest disagreement, Hui-neng is speaking to me and to you: "Don't think good; don't think evil." At this very moment, don't think parent or child, spouse or sibling, employee, race, straight or gay, or any role with which you and I might identify ourselves.

What is my original face?

It is as if we paint our delusions on a scrim hung between us and the world. On it we paint our roles and the ways we wish we were seen, in hope that others will see us that way. On it we paint images of the world as we wish to see it. When looking at my own scrim, I see a stereotype of myself. Tear down the scrim or not, the world is such, as it is. You are such, as you are, whether separate or not separate. Returning to the silence, to the poetry, without confusion of the concepts we have of self and other, now what is my face?

Bashō wrote these three poems:

> If seen by day,
> A firefly
> Is just a red-necked bug.
>
> —

The black crow I always despised,
And yet against the snowy dawn...

–

In the moonlight
There were flowers
But it was just a field of cotton.

Don't think mysterious dancing light of the firefly; don't think dull red-necked bug. As it is. Don't think despised black crow; don't think stunning contrast against white snow in dawn's light. Just crow.

There is another aspect of preconception we bring as well. In the face of suffering and injustice, it can seem impossible to be patient with the pace of change. We can demand the world and others around us meet our expectations in taking steps, to alleviate what we see as wrong and in the way; we see it can be done right now. Each day that passes multiplies the suffering and injustice. And the pace of change can be over millennia.

For me, development of patience to the pace of the world is an outgrowth of sitting with this one breath, one breath outside of time. I can't say what is your way. Each finding our way to hold the wrenching suffering is inescapable for any open heart. The more deeply piercing we feel the knife of suffering when considering an issue before our groups, big and small, the easier it can be to drift from righteous passion to self-righteousness without respectfulness.

We all want belonging, love, and respect, and it's seductive to reach for them by convincing others to agree with us. All with an open heart want to alleviate suffering, and it is seductive to reach for relief by convincing others to support our solution.

In the story of Hui-neng, the group includes the old teacher Hung-jen, head monk Ming, the illiterate barbarian Hui-neng, and the rest of the unnamed assembly. The koan begins before the first written line, in silence. Hung-jen is first to respond from the silence: To his age? To his own decline? We don't know. But he acts, likely recognizing the coming change to his status and apparently recognizing the drama that will unfold in the group. To act, he must be ready to lose what is dear to him—belonging, love, the integrity of the monastery in his care; all are at risk. But to act or not to act, change will occur as reflected in whatever motivated him to retire in the first place.

Hung-jen acted and in doing so risked being wrong. Perhaps he accepted that he might be a great Zen teacher but a lousy manager. He chose to require the public nature of his means of selection while aware of the jealousies in the group. Once the poems were offered, he knew what would arise if he didn't authorize Ming to teach, and the best response he could come up with for Hui-neng was to help him run away. Don't think good. Don't think evil. I row Hui-neng across the river.

There is a reasonable question that is also frequently a barrier to action: Is there a better choice?

If no action is taken, whether that non-action is remaining silent or speaking, nothing happens; the monastery lacks creative opportunity and is dead, not engaged in what is true. Through our days, each circumstance calls for a response that risks all—a call for action that is no action, like sleeping when tired. An example of no action that is action can occur when not asking someone we know if they are being abused. Each circumstance, whether obvious or not, is a chance to recognize one's deep response.

In the story, Ming is receptive to the question about offering his name and writing a poem. Doing so, he risks all. This action—write a poem—requires his readiness to be denigrated. And he was denigrated by Hung-jen's public refusal to offer the transmission that he thought was warranted.

Hui-neng was receptive to the question, asking what was going on, offering his own poem, and ready to be pilloried. He too was denigrated by the rest of the assembly.

The assembly was receptive to the question raised by Hung-jen; only two were drawn to offer poems. For the rest, no action that is action. The assembly was receptive to Hung-jen reporting he had already offered the robe and bowl to Hui-neng. The assembly acted: Restore the world we know; retrieve the robe and bowl!

It is worth noting that much of the fuel for this koan was provided by the response of all to the robe and bowl, symbols of transmission. In the imagery I've been using here, the robe and bowl are an image painted on the scrim. There was a robe and bowl that could be confounded with the experience of the opening and freedom accessible to us all. Similarly, Confederate statues were and are symbols that divide Americans. To some, these symbols mean racism. To others, history, a culture, and tradition. Each individual may perceive the other's perspective as disrespectful and dismissive, and thus deeply offensive. We have no end of objects that become divisive symbols, like gender-neutral bathrooms or hijabs. Receptiveness calls us to listen: What is true for the person before me? What meaning does this person find in this symbol? What does this symbol mean to me?

It is directly relevant that Hui-neng, the sixth patriarch, chose to let the tradition of robe and bowl as symbols of transmission die with him.

Once Ming caught up with Hui-neng, the reception and response unfolded with each action. Ming was open to his own mess of thoughts and feelings as he tried to lift the robe and bowl—and his inability to do so. Perhaps there was an anguished cry not written into our version. Perhaps a minute or a day went by. He abandoned the image of teacher he'd painted of himself on the scrim that he offered the world and accepted this action that is no action. "Help me! Teach me!" Think about what it would take to turn around and say, "Teach me," to the one you are most closed to. What would it take to bring such receptivity to yourself for your own closed heart, anger, and fear?

Ming responded with an open hand. What would change in those we met if we brought that attitude, that of seeing those we meet as our teacher? Or in any given moment, it may be the open hand missing is the one we offer ourselves. Am I listening to another without respecting the teacher in me?

In abandoning all else in this action, Ming was available to new experience. "Don't think good. Don't think evil." At this moment of jealousy, disappointment in myself, humiliation before my peers—all written in my expression—what is my original face? Leaving nothing out.

Without acting, without risking all, Ming would not have received the teaching that freed him.

This is the mess of community—in this case, in the form of jealousy and aggression. It is helpful to recognize that we endlessly paint images each on our own scrim, separating us from seeing simply what is, moment by moment. This rising endlessly implies that we cannot wait for our own delusion to stop before acting. If we expect that we can ourselves act always without the distortion of our own delusions, then that is an image of ourselves we have painted on the scrim. If we expect that others around us can or should act without delusion, then that is another image on the scrim.

The mild or impassioned tension that arises from a difference among us is calling us. Attention! When in our impassioned responses we range from righteous determination to address suffering and injustice, and from self-righteous indignation leading to separation of self and other, we are called. Attention! Whether we see or do not see, in Jewish tradition we are told in everything is the spark of the divine.

Kabir was a fifteenth-century Indian poet, born to a Muslim family, who was influenced by Sufi and Hindu traditions. He invites receptivity in this poem:

> Are you looking for me? I am in the next seat.
> My shoulder is against yours.
> You will not find me in the stupas, not in Indian

shrine rooms, nor in synagogues, nor in cathedrals:
not in masses, nor kirtans, not in legs winding
around your own neck, nor in eating nothing
    but vegetables.
When you really look for me, you will see me
instantly—
you will find me in the tiniest house of time.
Kabir says: Student, tell me, what is God?
He is the breath inside the breath.

In his life, Kabir was threatened by both Hindus and
Muslims, and in his death, he is claimed by both.

We can present as a firefly or a red-necked bug without
distinction—received as either firefly or dull bug. *What is*
can include feeling encouraged when received as a Firefly and
saddened when received as the Dull Bug. Likewise, we can
receive another as Firefly or Dull Bug in any moment, with
the resultant connection or tension likely to arise.

In the koan that tells the story of Hui-neng, passions are
extreme, actions taken, conflict undeniable, and respectfulness
lost. Yet, all is well. The mess along the way would have been
no one's ideal, but the opportunity arose again and again for
open eyes, for respectfulness at each moment.

Perhaps there is no messier discord than that of the Mid-
east, repeatedly leading to suffering, death, and seemingly ir-
reconcilable differences. Yet in 1978, President Carter helped
Israeli President Menachem Begin and Egyptian President
Anwar Sadat to find common ground and step toward peace.
Begin was a member of a militant group of fighters even before

there was a nation of Israel. Sadat was an army officer who engaged in war against Israel in 1967 and again when he was president in 1973.

The animosity between Begin and Sadat was profound, and they found a vision for peace, free from the fixed images of each other and each nation. Anwar Sadat was assassinated by officers of his own army in 1981 because of his participation in the peace accord. In 1993 Israeli Defense Minister and then later Prime Minister Yitzhak Rabin was similarly involved in the Oslo Peace Accord with Yasser Arafat. In 1995 Rabin was assassinated by a radical Orthodox Jew because of his involvement in the accord.

It is with sadness even now that I reflect on each being assassinated by those in the nations to which they were dedicated, demonstrating the differences within us are at least as profound as those among us. Designations of "us" and "them" become meaningless in a concrete way, even as they melt when concepts of self and other fall away.

There is space for weeping and anger within that which is. Openness to that which is inspires response. Suffering inspires passion. And all is well.

In my wrestling to open and respond to this troubled world, it has seemed that neither bowing nor accepting are enough. Taking a stand isn't enough. There is no safe stance or rule in discerning an appropriate response. I can and have erred in speaking, and can and have erred when not speaking.

In a prayer, Meister Eckhart said:

Apprehend God in all things, for God is in all things.
Every single creature is full of God and is a book
  about God.
Every creature is a word of God.
If I spent enough time with the tiniest creature—
  even a caterpillar—
I would never have to prepare a sermon.
So full of God is every creature.

And so, without excuse, we wrestle, with only receptivity to navigate to a response in accord. But receptivity to what? In what direction did Ming look? Or do you? Or do I?

I wish I could say I was grateful for the affronts of these past few years in evoking my wrestling with receptivity and response—and I do have some gratitude. I find it is my practice at every moment to open my eyes and see what is. It is my nature to see and to not see. In bringing receptiveness practice to my participation as a member of an assembly and of a nation, I bring intention to see those with whom I am in disagreement as thus, inexpressibly radiant. Disagreement can be steadfast in taking a stand. Disagreement can be consistent with the utter respectfulness of Ming's recognition of his own face as radiant while filthy, sweaty, and contorted. Disagreement can carry the respectfulness of Sadat and Begin at Camp David, Arafat and Rabin in Oslo, and me and you when we engage with attention to that which is.

It is with this respectfulness that I will stop writing here and invite you to your own receptivity.

9

Hurt, anger, forgiveness, and acceptance

I vow to see through

In Case 152 as told in *The True Dharma Eye: Dōgen's Three Hundred Koans,* Nanyang Huizhong has this exchange with the emperor of China:

> Nanyang arrived at the front of the palace with Emperor Suzong. Nanyang pointed at a figure of a stone lion and said to the emperor, "Your Majesty, this lion is extraordinary. Please say a turning word."
>
> Emperor Su said, "I cannot say anything. Will you please say something?"
>
> Nanyang said, "It is my fault."
>
> Later Danyuan Yingzhen asked Nanyang, "Did the emperor understand it?"
>
> Nanyang said, "Let's put aside whether the emperor understood it. How do you understand it?"

In reading the case with Nanyang and the emperor, I was captured by the simplicity of the statement, "It is my fault." In our daily lives it can be so easy to respond defensively to a perceived error or event or to apologize profusely. In the former, we can be righteous or indignant, ready to emphatically make sure we are understood. When profusely apologizing, we can easily feel diminished or fearful that we will be rejected for our error. But this is a Zen story that has remained since the Tang dynasty; Nanyang died in 775 CE. There must be more.

I found commentary about this koan that ascribed Nanyang's "It is my fault" to indicate that as teacher he took responsibility for Emperor Su having missed the point. Perhaps it was Nanyang's intention, but we can't know—and I find no vitality in this understanding. There must be more.

If offended, the emperor could have had Nanyang killed; Nanyang's response could have been self-preservation. That could be true, but again would lack vitality to have preserved the story through the years. Also, the story begins with Nanyang calling for a *turning word* from the emperor—a response beyond ordinary and extraordinary. Even if one of these possibilities I describe as lacking in vitality is true, we benefit from using the story to recognize our own turning word outside of taking or assigning fault.

I know from having presented this chapter as a talk that there are many whose life experiences make it difficult to read this without overemphasizing self-fault. As you read, please be as open as you can to find another way to hold this. In the phrase, "It is my fault," all four words are fraught. To what does *it* refer? Who is referenced by *my*? This is a Zen story; is there an observation of a *fault* here beyond right and wrong?

With perception of things said and done in person-to-person interactions, hurt, anger, and blame arise. With such reactions there is the potential for forgiveness and acceptance that includes hurt and anger. Blame can take us beyond anger to contempt and hatred, and when it does, we lose the entwining of *I am* and *we,* and we lose empathy.

I suspect we all know what it feels like when we recognize we really blew it. We let ourselves or someone else down, or hurt someone. Even thinking about it might evoke cringing and heaviness. Sometimes all it takes is a memory of something we said or did years ago to bring back that regret. Where is Zen practice while we cringe?

Similarly, we all know what it feels like to be angry, if not furious, with someone who hurt us or let us down, or who misunderstood our intent completely and dismisses or refuses to listen to the clarification we are offering. The transgression could have been years ago, but if it still hurts, it might also still bring anger now. Where is Zen practice in this anger?

The koan that is forgiveness and acceptance took hold of me when I first started working with survivors of unhealthy spiritual communities. I use the cumbersome *unhealthy spiritual communities* rather than the more clear and concise word *cults* because many of the groups that traumatized the people I know were on a continuum of connection to mainstream religions. In meeting people where they are, I honor their own identification of their experience as being *cult, cult-like,* or *unhealthy.*

I learned that when in the religious community my friends and clients later recognized as unhealthy, individuals were taught that their only chance for redemption was through the specific beliefs and practices of the group. Folks left when they no longer believed the doctrine. But I heard almost universally that what remained when they walked away was the sense of damnation (contempt), no longer with any means of redemption (acceptance).

I am moved when seeing that for survivors of unhealthy spiritual communities, and for all of us, how painful and persistent our judgment of self and others can be. I don't see this as a flaw. I do see this tendency as a call to address the koan of forgiveness and acceptance.

Anger and forgiveness are inherent aspects of our practice, though we may not focus on them often. In Three Treasures Sangha, we regularly chant the Four Infinite Vows, including the second vow:

Blind passions without cease, I vow to see through.

That is the current version in use, translated by Jack Duffy some years ago. Three Treasures Sangha had used earlier translations by Robert Aitken which also changed over time. The evolution of the translations is relevant to the topic at hand. When I first came to Three Treasures Sangha, we used this translation:

Delusion is inexhaustible; I vow to cut it off.

After Aitken modified it, the sangha chanted this version:

> Greed, anger, and ignorance rise endlessly; I vow to
> abandon them.

Aitken once again modified his own earlier translation, in which he replaced *anger* with *hatred.* The next version read:

> Greed, hatred, and ignorance rise endlessly; I vow to
> abandon them.

Over time, the emphasis in the translations has moved through *cut off* to *abandon* and *see through.* In this, I perceive a shift from fighting against inexhaustible delusions to choosing the direction of attention. Or we could say the shift invited us to open our eyes wider in recognition of all that arises, even the most troublesome of sensations. In these shifts, there is a difference of attitude, with *seeing through* and *abandonment* requiring no rejection. And we apparently no longer vow to abandon *anger,* but do vow to abandon *hatred.*

Another sutra the Three Treasures Sangha regularly chants is currently titled Purification. When I first joined the sangha, it was titled Repentance and went like this:

> All the evil karma, ever created by me since of old,
> on account of my beginningless greed, anger and
> ignorance,
> Born of my conduct, speech, and thought,
> I now confess openly and fully.

By 2013, the title of the version in our sutra book became Purification and included a new second line, changing only the word *anger* to now read:

> ...on account of my beginningless greed, hatred and
> ignorance...

Again we've moved away from the need to purify and confess our anger, and instead we purify and confess our hatred.

We are Zen practitioners, and here I am filling the air with loaded, complicated words like *confess, purification, forgive, anger,* and *hatred.* Each word represents an attempt to communicate a human experience we all share, but which is not the experience itself, and we may not be using the words in the same way. Let's be very careful. Remember also that most of these words are already used in our tradition, sutras, talks, and discussion. It is fitting that we find these words in our place of practice, where we have space for all that is, because surely these words have places in our lives.

In Ann Arbor, I lived by a church that changed the sayings on their marquee weekly. The only one I remember: "Anger is like burning down your own house to get rid of a rat." I recall this saying for the clear expression of aspects of anger. First, anger is an emotion that can be very unsettling to the one who is angry as well as to those hearing it! Second, we still don't want the rat in the house. If we are too quick to extinguish, cut off, or even abandon anger, we risk losing the message it carried: Get rid of the rat! And *now* would be good!

A dharma brother, who was present with Aitken Roshi in Honolulu when the translation changes to these sutras were made, told me that Aitken remembered his own Japanese teacher's righteous anger at the lifeless state of Zen in Japan at the time. Aitken changed the word *anger* to *hatred* out of respect for his teacher and the worthwhile role of anger. Worthwhile or not, anger is also a human emotion that arises sometimes in all of, as do disappointment and joy. How can we recognize all that is and also cut off and abandon human emotion? We may as well try to cut off seeing the color green.

Still, I want you to know how I am using the words, so I'll do so with a story.

Some years ago, my friend Joe and I were to meet at a house he had never been to. I didn't know the address but described where it was on a street and said it was the one with vertical redwood siding. I don't think about color when giving a description, since I'm color blind. I was a carpenter at the time, and thought I was telling him the type of wood siding on the house. When Joe arrived about forty-five minutes late, I learned the house was green. He threw a very expressive tantrum, grunting, growling, dropping to his knees, with elbows bent and fists clenched, crying out skyward with his frustration. I was of course apologetic and felt terrible! I was also amazed—he expressed his anger and frustration with absolute abandon, and nothing was directed at me. He was just angry—and for the sake of our vocabulary today—with no hatred. I did not feel separate from Joe or his anger; we shared the experience. If he expressed hatred, even briefly, there would have been us and them and taking sides, in opposition rather than allied.

I want to speak concretely about practice with anger and forgiveness; to do so I'll make up an example that is a composite of things I've heard and lived. Blake and Taylor have been very close for a long time. They share a living space, and each has areas of a kitchen counter for things they individually use.

Blake gave Taylor a gift of a lovely organizer so Taylor could neatly arrange things in their area. Taylor used part of the organizer and put part away, only to return home one day and find that Blake had reorganized Taylor's area. Taken aback, Taylor complained about Blake changing their system. Blake explained that they were trying to help. Both became heated, angry, speaking hurtfully and being hurt. History arose. On the one side: Why are you always moving my stuff? There is no room for me here! And on the other side: Why do you have to get so angry so fast! You didn't appreciate my gift and put it away!

I've painted a generic scene that captures an experience I remember too well. The content—stuff on a counter—is trivial. But the actions represent something not trivial, very human, and tender. Living in moments such as this one, I'm hurt and angry, I want what I say to be acknowledged. I might care for the person with whom I am struggling, but I'm not aware of it in the moment; I need to protect myself. At such moments, it's as if we live in a castle and just put down the portcullis and lifted the bridge over the moat. We're safe from invaders, weapons in hand at the battlements. Where is receptivity now?

Nanyang said, "It is my fault."

A leaf falls in the water of a quiet pond; ripples spread in all directions. It is my fault.

Wind blows a leaf free from a tree; the leaf falls on a pond and ripples spread. It is my fault.

A tree grows near a pond; a leaf's attachment to the branch weakens with the season. It is my fault.

What does the *my* in *my fault* mean? Too many of us have learned to doubt ourselves as we are. When doubting, it is difficult to recognize the breadth of fault arising from the dance of seasons, wind, and leaf all inextricably part of one dance of life.

Who is this *my* in *my fault?* Is it pond, leaf, tree, season, or wind? For your circumstances, try asking the questions from within the unbounded web of life. Or maybe it's more useful to turn the question around and ask: Who and what are not at fault and not involved?

The dance without beginning or end includes responsibility that is also embedded within our histories, the histories of our parents, their parents, and all that has come before. Every moment and every deed, good and bad, calls for our compassion. There is a place to stand in loving, accepting embrace of just this.

None of this conflicts with personal responsibilities for the actions we've taken and will take. In the context of acceptance and compassion, we recognize responsibility, and respond to this too, in accord. The Boddhisatva Precepts stand with us, to guide our ethical behavior along the Way. When all is taken within the warmth of compassion, Buddha nature is undimmed.

I was once waiting to testify in court as an expert witness in a civil case when the judge paused the case to hear a criminal matter that took precedent. The criminal defendant was charged with armed robbery of a convenience store, with all the unfortunate circumstances of the event and his life. After the hearing was over, a colleague turned to me and said, "When I've walked into a 7-Eleven, it never occurred to me to wonder, 'Should I rob this place?'" I laughed at the time; it seemed so ludicrous for either of us. That it was ludicrous was more likely due to circumstances than our virtue.

Thinking of it now, my colleague's comment gave proportionality to questions of our taking and asking another to take responsibility. For most of us, most of the time, the issues are modest. We can otherwise easily let our conversations about acceptance, forgiveness, and responsibility be skewed by the extremes of sexual predators, violent criminals, and robber barons. If skewed, we can be distracted by fear of being imperfect and therefore horrible, or anger that one we love is imperfect and therefore horrible.

In this understanding of Nanyang, there is no resistance and no separation. I am hurt and angry, closing off the world in my castle. It is my fault. Nanyang need not fall on his sword with shame that he is not more or different, and he need not struggle against another or the world because the other should be more or different. The leaf falls, ripples spread. I'm hurt; I can't really open my heart mind to listen to you right now. I need safety.

In the ideal, recognizing no separation and no self other than who I am in this very circumstance, I would wish to feel "Zen" about it—using "Zen" to mean even tempered, as it is used in the vernacular. Very nice of course. But as we sit behind walls, protecting and attacking, being "Zen" is also present even here. Otherwise we are in the ironic position of lacking equanimity about lacking equanimity.

The simplicity of *It is my fault* can include *I am hurt and my heart is closed.* Or it can include *I am angry and I said hurtful things.* Just the practice of receptivity can be profound. Opening to *what is* requires we set down the struggle to be more. It can also mean the release of struggle against being less than the standard to which we hold ourselves, and thus accept the risk of our being perceived as worthless.

There is a koan I heard once in which a student (who later became the teacher Ikkyū) asked the master to tell him about impermanence. The teacher explained that all things change; we cannot avoid loss. The student said, "Thank you, that's comforting because I just broke your favorite tea bowl."

This student missed something here. In acceptance, there is still room for sorrow and an apology. We vow to abandon greed, hatred, and ignorance—which is different from vowing to never be greedy, hateful, or ignorant. Confessing openly and fully that I said mean things can purify. And for this student, beginning with a confession about breaking the favored tea bowl could have been an honest expression of no more and no less, and of regret and remorse. If fearing that being less defines us as such, it's difficult to reveal ourselves when being less in this fleeting moment.

To do so asks that we release ideas of self, namely releasing expectations that I do not say mean things, or that I would not, because I'm a caring and thoughtful person. We can't very well release ideas of self when we protect ourselves behind walls, and we can't tolerate opening the gates to these walls unless feeling some degree of safety. Here is a starting point to practice. Here is the practice of no-self, in the messiness that relationship can bring out.

"I am not yet ready to open the gates" is a confession too, a recognition of the truth of who one is now. Receptivity is nowhere other than right here. "I am not yet ready to open and forgive" is another confession to myself or to another. This no-self we talk about is not a distant concept; it is available in this confession—this simple acknowledgment—of what is.

It is also easy to get lost in what it means to forgive—and that it might not mean the same to me as it does to you.

Here are three meanings I found for the word *forgive:* To give up expectation of restitution or accountability; to cease to bear resentment; to pardon or determine there was never an act requiring forgiveness. None of these meanings requires that we forget. Each describes a different experience for the one forgiving and for the one to whom forgiveness is offered. The three together allow for a matrix of hurt feelings and resentments for us when we're involved in this.

One example would arise if you pardon or absolve me, believing you expected too much of me, so you conclude there was no fault on my part after all. If I am hurt by your perception of my limited capacity, I carry that. But bringing it back to Zen practice, who is it that carries the hurt and where is it carried to?

Asked another way, what does it mean to *see through* this hurt and the web of these feelings?

Ours is a practice of joining with what is. *What is* can include sorrow for one's own error and thoughtfulness about doing otherwise in the future. *What is* can include protecting oneself from being in a position to be hurt by another in the future. With compassion and openness to *what is,* there is room for the recognition necessary for purification. Responding appropriately to *what is* can include listening to anger, sorrow, regret, guilt. Now what is a fitting response?

Maybe it's an artifact of my engineering work in the field of failure analysis such that I find context and deeper understanding in the extremes of things. In engineering, we don't really understand a system until we know how it breaks down. Failure is not a bad word; rather, it is inevitable, and it provides data about limits. Maybe that's why I find the poignancy of Simon Wiesenthal's concentration camp reflections on forgiveness and acceptance to be compelling and directly relevant to me, and I hope to you, too.

While still in a Nazi concentration camp, Simon Wiesenthal was randomly taken off a work crew to hear the confession of a young SS officer dying from burns. His face was wrapped and not visible. The SS officer told of shooting Jewish men, women, and children as they fled a building that had caught fire from the grenades he and others threw inside. Quoting from Wiesenthal's story:

> The officer said, "Behind the windows of the second floor, I saw a man with a small child in his arms. His clothes were alight. By his side stood a woman, doubtless the mother of the child. With his free hand the man covered the child's eyes...then he jumped into the street...I don't know how many tried to jump out of the windows, but that one family I shall never forget—least of all the child. It had black hair and dark eyes...

Wiesenthal remained silent, unable to forgive the man, but carried the image for years, also unable to accept or perhaps forgive his own choice. The question of his actions became Wiesenthal's koan. In the book he wrote to work through this persistent question, he ended by asking the reader to change places with him in that hospital room and consider, "What would I have done?"

After all the horror of the concentration camps, Wiesenthal carried this question of his silence with the SS officer for years, chewing it. His silence in that hospital room was a response, but not his only response. He allowed the officer to take his hand, and Wiesenthal remained there holding the hand while repulsed by the story the officer told. He also visited the young man's mother after the war, saw his face in pictures, and heard her grief for the boy who was so devout before Germany was swept by the insanity that was and is Nazism. And Wiesenthal was silent again, when he could have told the grieving mother more of what her boy had done.

After Wiesenthal's story, the book continues with essays addressing his question, written by Jews and Christians, artists and philosophers, and survivors of holocausts (plural). One of the essays was written by Jean Améry, another survivor of Nazi concentration camps. Améry addressed the fluidity and ephemeral nature of our capacity for forgiveness:

> If I had been in such a situation, perhaps I would have been more yielding. Both your intransigence and my magnanimity...would mean nothing to me.

...forgiving or not forgiving in this specific case is nothing more than a question of temperament or feeling. I do not want to impute any other possible behavior to you, but I can easily imagine that, under only slightly different circumstances you might have forgiven the dying man. Suppose you had seen his pleading and imploring eyes, which may have had more of an effect on you than his rasping voice and folded hands. Or suppose that before that encounter, you had been in contact with one of those "decent" SS men, whom we all knew, who had treated you with a little bit of kindness, putting you in a more tolerant mood...So, then you might have forgiven: in my view it would have meant just as little as your (or possibly my) refusal.

Open to *what is,* it is my fault. Forgiveness or not forgiveness, it is my fault.

If Wiesenthal resolved the question for himself, it was not shown in his book nor in the reprints. I trust with full engagement in humanity, the discomfort of joining his hand with that of the murderous, repentant, and bereft SS officer broke down the separateness we sometimes would prefer. Who of us wants to find how much we share with those who we call monsters? Now the koan of forgiveness cuts both ways.

How about for the anger, hatred, regret, grave errors, and valid grievances you carry today? How about the anger you felt, feel, and will feel when arguing with someone dear to you—perhaps triggered by something small but having meaning that is penetrating you? I would not presume to give answers. But you can take it as a koan, calling for your response. In Wiesenthal's and Amery's responses, we see there is not only one way. In grappling with our own koan of anger, hatred, forgiveness, and acceptance, there is one way—your response in accord.

When behind the protective walls of our anger, here is a place to begin. Openly and fully—without barrier to what is, even now.

Returning to Purification:

> All the evil karma, ever created by me since of old,
> on account of my beginningless greed, hatred and ignorance,
> Born of my conduct, speech, and thought,
> I now confess openly and fully.

Openly and fully—without barrier to *what is,* even now.

I'll finish with a quote from Desmond Tutu, written to explain Ubuntu, the principle central to the healing manifest through the Truth and Reconciliation Commission:

> My humanity is inextricably bound up in yours. We belong in a bundle of life.

10
Why does it come to this?

I vow to free

From *The Record of Tung Shan* (the teacher also known as Dongshan Liangjie), Koan Case 98 goes like this:

> One time when the Master was washing his bowls, he saw two birds contending over a frog.
>
> A monk who also saw this asked, "Why does it come to that?"
>
> The Master replied, "It's only for your benefit, Ācārya."

For a time at our Three Treasures Sangha, before sitting we took up the translations of the first of the Four Infinite Vows, also known as the Bodhisattva Vows. The version translated by Jack Duffy in the Three Treasures Sangha sutra book is:

> All beings beyond number, I vow to free.

Aitken Roshi's translation, titled Great Vows for All, differs:

> The many beings are numberless;
> I vow to save them.

In striving over the frog, the birds act on their vow to free us. The frog offers its life to free us. Each calls to us to release craving, release choosing. Releasing all ambitions and expectations, I am free to speak; I am free to nap. Each of these koans—of the birds and frog, and the first Infinite Vow— is one side of the same reversible garment.

Birds and frog provide for us the immediacy, cutting through abstract expressions to vitalize the first Noble Truth about illness and death: Why does it come to torment? The first Noble Truth is the recognition of suffering as innate to existence. Not necessarily constant for you or me in a given moment, but doubtlessly inescapable over our days, and never a moment is this world absent of suffering.

My co-teacher, Madelon, helped me by finding another translation that speaks for me. In the one above, the monk asked, "Why does it come to that?" Here is the other version:

> Once when Master Dongshan was washing his bowls with another monk, they both saw two birds contending over a frog. The monk asked, "Why does it have to come to this?"
>
> The master said, "It's only for your benefit, venerable."

A small thing, but for me the word *this* is closer, more intimate. When what we see comes to *this,* undeniable and visceral, we are given the gift of fire, of motivation. Why *this?* Why here, now? As if a demand to Stop! See!

The second Noble Truth is that suffering arises from craving, from attachment. The third Noble Truth states that suffering can end through letting go.

That fire of motivation may be valid as far as it goes, as in the saying that we listen to reason but we obey pain. Beyond motivation, *this* calls to us before thought, before the story of how all the pieces fit. It calls us to see what we see and hear what we hear. That call is unlimited, available as you are reading, even now.

Days before writing this, I went to dinner on Capitol Hill in Seattle. It was early in the time of Covid and not long after the death of George Floyd. I parked near fire trucks that blocked the street beyond the next intersection, lights flashing. The kiosks to pay for parking were all smashed, their glass cracked, and were posted with warnings about the safety of leaving a car in this area. Police cars and police abounded. Smoke rose from somewhere on the next block, perhaps from a fire that had been set. On the street were spectators craning to see what was going on. We all could hear the chants of protestors.

There were police and there were protestors. How would you count? Was it two bodies? Or one in isometric exercise?

Reaching the Plum Bistro, I sat at a table against the sidewalk where the whole wall was open, rolled up to the ceiling. I heard what I hoped was a flash bang, though I wouldn't know to distinguish the sound of a gun. Sirens and more lights flashed, reflected off windows with the passing of an AMR ambulance. Was this one motion of injured and ambulance? Or two?

Spectators watched on the sidelines, face masks on. A garbage truck stopped, and cars flowed around it with varying patience. People were parking, getting in and out of on-demand rides, greeting others, and going in and out of buildings and restaurants. Some seemed to walk toward the protests. Most went about their evening in high spirits as if all in this scene were routine, which I knew it had become for this neighborhood. As one sangha member reminded us when we were discussing the opening koan about the birds and frog: "It's not all frog guts." One city was finding its way on a Saturday night, with me in that undertow, being drawn into *this,* one city, one night, one body. All pieces playing one Big Band song, the discordant phrases shocking us listeners to cringe away.

All beings beyond number. I have vowed to free, to save.

The garbage truck blocked the street traffic and my view beyond the sidewalk while its single worker was noisily saving all while collecting the containers from an unseen location. The restaurant server was saving me as he set my plates on the table. My eating was a compassionate act for body and mind after a week of work isolated at home. We may each have a different view on what actions are compassionate service and which are blind and self-serving. When compassionate, protesters declare for the needs of those in need. When compassionate, police declare for the protection of others, for order on behalf of all.

I know police who see their work as service and who have wept when subjected to stones and angry debasement. As a protester, I've been chased, treated roughly, and teargassed by angry police. Each event in the news seems to be accompanied by blame—and not just related to police and protests. Is it more in our culture than others that we question unremittingly who was responsible? As if nothing should ever go wrong, as if each loss was avoidable and should be avoided the next time?

During a community discussion of this koan story, one member observed that neither Master Dongshan nor the other monk expressed blame or guilt in seeing what they saw. Yet there was no barrier to their embrace of *this* before them.

In a relevant poem, the poet Stonehouse adds commentary to the subject:

> Scorpion tails and wolf hearts pervade the world
> everyone has a trick to get ahead
> but how many smiles in a lifetime
> or moments of peace in a day
> who can change tracks when their cart tips over
> when disaster strikes there's no time for shame
> this old monk isn't merely pointing fingers
> he's trying to remove people's blinders and chains

The garbage truck itself rises with mechanical roars and bangs to save us. No less so, the man entering the restaurant while pulling on his face mask responds to the first Infinite Vow during the time of pandemic. Sometimes though, we hear the call all the more when it seems unbearable to us, and we cannot help but call out, like the monk: Why does it come to this?

That evening on Capitol Hill, the intersection at Twelfth Avenue and Pike was the ancient way, and still is, as the street before my house now is the ancient way I walk today. Just as you walk the ancient way with every step in kinhin.

In a lecture by Dōgen, the influential thirteenth-century Japanese master, he recalled a story:

> ...a monk asked Yün-men, "How is it when it is expressed completely in a single phrase?"

Yün-men said, "Ripped apart from ancient times till now."

Each of us with compassionate receptivity hears the cries of the world; each of us is naked before the undeniable facts. How do I and how do you respond now, ripped apart as we are? Don't forget your own cries. Attention! Respond!

We toil to protect what we love, to protect what is vital, to soothe agony, and to evoke joy. All that is vital passes quickly away; all agony too passes quickly away. Also undeniable is that which is here, numberless beings in our toil, playing one song, from ancient times till now, animating the first of the Great Vows for All:

> The many beings are numberless,
> I vow to save them.

The vow is a koan indeed; there is more than the words can convey—words such as *many, numberless, I, save, them*. The vow is wonderful as written, and each of these words is uneven ground to trip us.

I looked up "free" in the *Oxford English Dictionary* and found this definition: "not or no longer in servitude," "Not subject to the control or influence of something abstract," ; and from old English, "Not impeded, restrained, or restricted in actions, activity, or movement.

We can understand the vow to save, to free, with conventional language, and rightly so. Master Dōgen spoke for the benefit of others in the circumstances of his time, and would

find no conflict in our doing so today, as recorded in this
passage of his words:

> If you make a vow not to see a woman for ages and ages
> to come, won't you be neglecting them when you vow,
> "Sentient beings are numberless; I vow to save them"?
> If you neglect them, you are no bodhisattva. Is this
> the great compassion of the Buddha? This vow is the
> raving of a drunkard who has drunk deeply from the
> wine barrel of the small vehicle.

Our vows are now and have always been more than practice on the cushion, not limited to the count of a breath, the
sound in a room. Otherwise, neither the monk nor Dongshan
would have raised their gaze to observe birds and frog.

But to stop there is to disembowel Zen practice, as if freeing
is dependent on circumstances. Stopping here is to stumble
on the ground of the words and ideas. In *Shobogenzo,* Dōgen
wrote these two passages:

> When one thing becomes a Buddha, all things become
> Buddhas. When Shakyamuni attained enlightenment,
> he said, "When the morning star appeared, I and the
> great earth with all its beings simultaneously became
> Buddhas."...What we call the body and mind in the
> Buddha Way is grass, trees, and wall rubble; it is wind,
> rain, water, and fire.

I might add flash bangs and garbage trucks to Dōgen's list,
as well as sound and video freezing and unfreezing over Zoom.

And another passage from Dōgen is this, as translated in
The Eastern Buddhist:

You only attain the mind of Buddha when there is no hating and no desiring. But do not try to gauge it with your mind or speak it with words. When you simply release and forget both your body and mind and throw yourself into the house of Buddha, and when functioning comes from the direction of Buddha and you go in accord with it, then with no strength needed and no thought expended, freed from birth and death, you become Buddha.

I am grateful for Dōgen's fine words, but they are dead unless we find their pulse in our arms today. And to appreciate the pulse, we must avoid stumbling on these words. So let me speak as plainly as I can.

We cannot but have our own laments in seeing it has come to *this.* Our humanity cries out: "Why?" "How do I live in this world?" In our casting about, against our will, we vow: Save me. Save you. Save all. Sometimes in gratitude, sometimes in desperation, letting go, we see what we see and hear what we hear. In seeing and hearing, response arises without effort, in accord.

Responses arise, too, when we rejoice in the fall of light through a tree and the sight of the city softened by fog.

If there is anything of those few sentences that can be denied, I don't know it. If you can deny any of this, speak. We have already lamented and vowed. That leaves it to us to simply see what we see and hear what we hear. Without delay or hesitation, we can start now.

I'll leave you with a poem of Dōgen's:

What can I accomplish?
Although not yet a Buddha,
Let my priest's body
Be the raft to carry
Sentient beings to the yonder shore.

11
Engaging the Precepts

Do no harm, practice all good, save all beings

Dualistic responses abound around us, among us and within us. Hate crimes rose steadily from 2010–2019 while crime in general dropped. Hate crimes then rose faster yet during the Covid years. But perhaps these times are not unusual in the course of human history.

The Buddhist Precepts were not written for a specific time in history: They were written because we are human. Further affirming the universality of what we speak, the Precepts are also not unique. During Yom Kippur, the traditional prayer of forgiveness, Al Chet, is recited numerous times in each synagogue around the world. Al Chet includes recognition of sins akin in spirit to our own Precepts, about speaking falsely, exploitation, malice, hate, and others. Even in sincere practice, we can be blind and can benefit from specific reminders about things we do and don't do that can adversely affect those around us.

In our lineage, during the jukai ceremony we take the sixteen Bodhisattva Precepts, which include taking refuge in

Buddha, Dharma, and Sangha, the Three Pure Precepts, and the Ten Grave Precepts.

The Ten Grave Precepts in our sutra book are:

I take up the Way of Not Killing.

I take up the Way of Not Stealing.

I take up the Way of Not Misusing Sex.

I take up the Way of Not Speaking Falsely.

I take up the Way of Not Giving or Taking Drugs.

I take up the Way of Not Discussing Faults of Others.

I take up the Way of Not Praising Myself while Abusing Others.

I take up the Way of Not Sparing the Dharma Assets.

I take up the Way of Not Indulging in Anger.

I take up the Way of Not Defaming the Three Treasures.

The Three Pure Precepts in our sutra book are:

I vow to maintain the Precepts.

I vow to practice all good dharmas.

I vow to save the many beings.

I have only the deepest respect for the generosity, integrity, and intentions of all the people I know in Three Treasures Sangha and the Diamond Sangha. Thus, the application of Precepts in our settings requires a more nuanced consideration. In our lineage and beyond, each of us can benefit from reflection on engagement with the Precepts, to benefit all beings, and to manifest practice in this very moment. Each Precept is rich and could well be the subject of its own chapter. In this chapter, I will look more generally at the practice of the Precepts as koans and how we can hold and savor them.

I don't write this as an expert on relationship or the Precepts—that would be presumptuous. I saw one study of 417 ethicists who could be said to be experts, though they did not behave more ethically than others. I write this because of the importance of the subject, particularly for us as Zen practitioners.

I told this story briefly in an earlier chapter, but I want to look at it from another angle here. When Ikkyū was a young attendant to his teacher, he accidentally broke a rare and beautiful tea bowl of his master's. Hiding the pieces behind him, he asked his master to help him understand impermanence. His master explained that death is inevitable, and all things have limited life. Ikkyū revealed the broken cup and said that was good to know, because he had broken his master's favorite cup.

This story is not subtle, but our own similar misuses of Zen can arise in ways that can fool us. The Precepts stand to help us join acceptance of *what is* with ethical behavior. In the lineage of Three Treasures Sangha, we often meet the Precepts early when taking jukai and again at the end of the koan curriculum, to foster understanding, both practical and subtle, in the indivisible realms of form and emptiness. Being utterly human, together we reflect on the application of Precepts to our practice in relationship. We need each other to help us see what is in our own shadow.

The daily news is replete with examples of violations of the intentions of the Ten Grave Precepts. Starting at the top, taking the way of not killing stands out, with mass killings repeatedly fresh in all our minds. Whether or not killing directly, many actions can be indirectly detrimental to life through fostering poverty, climate disruption, divisive anger, and discussion of the faults of others. Taking up the way of not killing is indeed a subtle, wonderful, and necessary practice. It is a practice that is not far away from any of us, even as we sit and speak.

The Three Pure Precepts themselves are comprehensive. In the first of the Three Pure Precepts, we embrace all Precepts and vow to avoid harm to all beings in the many ways possible. The second Pure Precept is affirmative; in addition to the avoidance of harmful behaviors, we practice all good. The Precept includes no restriction on our creativity in understanding or acting to benefit this vast world. In the third Pure Precept, we commit to the liberation of all.

With the commitment to liberate all beings, we are reminded that we are not talking about someone else when we are offended by the lack of civility, violence, and threat of violence. If contemptuous of divisiveness, we are divided, and in fact, we are acting divisively. The more acrid the atmosphere, the more imperative that we examine in detail and renew our vow to save all beings—now, leaving no one and nothing separate. Any time we perceive others breaking the Precepts, we are called back to the third Pure Precept: Saving all beings leaves no one and nothing separate. I have not found this to be easy in recent years.

Holding the Precepts is also practice itself. Just as in kinhin, after the sound of the clapper, we walk toward our seats and take this step with nowhere to go. We hold intentions of moral behaviors and there is no one to behave morally. This is not amnesty or pardon for harmful behavior. We can drive freely about the world, operating within the painted lines and laws of the road. It is miraculous how well millions of people seamlessly drive a few feet apart and, for the benefit of all, trust and adhere to the lane markings. There is no contradiction between freedom and lawful driving. Holding the Precepts is no different.

My old friend and colleague Bruce visited not long ago. His unusual example inspired reflection on the subtlety of daily ethical choices we all face. Bruce owns a car that has not left his driveway for twelve years because he bikes and uses public transportation instead. He wastes little that I could see. He ate spoiled food, avoided napkins, and repaired materials whenever possible. I wrote about the trade-offs he was willing to make, which I thought reflected his commitment to a small carbon footprint and to taking up the way of not killing on a global scale through the smallest of actions. When I showed what I wrote to Bruce for his comments and permission to use the story, I found I had not fully understood my friend after all.

He did not perceive sacrifice in his choices, and his choices were based on many factors beyond climate change. For our purposes, it led me to consider that the same is likely true for all of us. Even our reasons for taking up a Precept can include deeply individual factors. Let us not be confused by the complexity of taking up the Precepts however, and thus miss their simplicity. I take up the way of not killing.

Yet we all must draw a line, here and now. In knowing Bruce, I could not help but reconsider my own choices each day: Showering in hot water—for how long? Driving to work—or walking, at what cost to arthritic joints? Disposing of food that had lost its appeal days before—while not fully spoiled?

In one 2018 study, making $32,400 or more in a year fell under the category of the top 1 percent of income worldwide. At times everyone uses resources indiscreetly. Where is the line between excess and asceticism? Where is the Middle Way? With consideration of other Precepts, at times everyone talks unkindly about another individual or group. Where is the line between being unkind and trying to better understand uncomfortable feelings about another through conversation? At times, everyone chooses to deaden their feelings. Where is the line between deadening and just rejuvenating? I don't know how to find the Middle Way without blundering over the line to one side and the other. That blundering is our humanity too. Each error joins us with all beings, in fear and courage, blindness and sight, inviting us to join just as we are.

At one time, I was working as a building contractor. A skilled friend and colleague, I'll call him Jules, was working for me as he completed his graduate degree at University of Michigan. Jules told me a particular job was complete, so I called for a building inspection. The city inspector said from the attic he could see light around one wall vent that needed caulking from the outside. Following up, I asked Jules to take care of it, and he said he went to the building and completed the small task. Once again, I called the inspector, who returned and told me the task wasn't done, and was much as he'd seen it before.

Mystified, I met with Jules. The task was simple, unambiguous. The only thing to be done on the site was a few minutes of caulking. What could the misunderstanding possibly have been? Jules was immediately remorseful. The building site was unusual in that there was a retaining wall a few feet from the basement, so the basement had daylight. That meant the ladder would be placed on top of the retaining wall at first-floor level. Jules, climbing that ladder to the place the needed caulking, would be three and a half stories above the ground. Jules said, "I'm so sorry, Lee. I set up the ladder. I couldn't face that climb, that drop, and I was so ashamed I couldn't tell you." Still bewildered and knowing Jules was intelligent, I said that he had to know I had to call the inspector and would find out. He said, "I was aware of that, and I still couldn't face it." He went on to say, "I hope this doesn't change your trust or respect for me going forward."

I'm grateful still to that long drop and to Jules for his candor. Both help me to understand taking up the way of not speaking falsely. Because of my respect for Jules, it was clear to me there was no evil in his lie to me, only his tenderness. This is what happens when the circumstances are more challenging than our capacity to meet them. Carl Jung cautioned that we tie ourselves in knots when trying to avoid necessary pain, a fine description of Jules and the caulking. And we all have our limits; I can't deny that I am Jules too. When we are unable to act on our intention to follow the Precepts, rather than deriding ourselves or each other, we can appreciate humanity being revealed. When in one hand we nestle the Precept of not speaking falsely with the Precept of saving all beings, intention and tenderness meet without conflict and join us in this world that leaves nothing out. We can hold these seamlessly together when setting aside the mind that parses and picks.

Certainly, we have life-scale choices about our commitment to living ethically, generously. There are also the choices that arise moment by moment. As practice, the question is not only about making ethical choices, but the spirit with which we make them. The way to definitively minimize our carbon footprint is to physically die now and cease the use of resources. In my friend Bruce's response to me about my perception of his asceticism, he quoted a Harvard professor who wrote a book about cycling and the environment. The author argued that cycling has a negative environmental impact because the exercise results in people living longer and therefore consuming more energy and resources. He proposed the best thing we could do for the environment would be to take up smoking and die sooner. Taken to the extreme, one could take this to say that taking up the way of not killing means to foster one's own or other humans' deaths.

Clearly this is internally inconsistent. Taking up smoking to shorten life falls short of practicing all good and is separate from saving all beings, right here, leaving none out. In minimizing carbon footprint, what use is there for art, cuisine, dance, or travelling even a small distance for any of the above?

Such contradictions, the scale of world problems, and the insignificance of our efforts can hobble our actions—through complacency and despair, however understandable—to practice all good calls for another response to such despair.

To include all of the Three Pure Precepts, discernment is necessary. Discernment includes the letter and the spirit of the Precepts; embracing the letter and spirit includes consideration of behaviors, their helpful and harmful effects, and the emptiness of all. The emptiness of all includes no death, no avoidance of death, no Precepts, and no avoidance of Precepts. This can't be done using ordinary language and perspectives.

We have wonderful examples of discernment in our traditions, including the well-known story of Thich Nath Hanh's poem, "Please Call Me by My True Names," from the book *Call Me By My True Names: The Collected Poems of Thich Nhat Hanh*. I won't include the story or the poem here, because I expect many readers already know it well. (Or see the small excerpt from the poem in the next chapter.) It is a story that unfailingly moves me, carrying me through Thich Nath Hanh's own anger at the brutal acts of pirates, to his dropping blindness to his own piracy and barriers to his own compassion.

Embracing all, there is also no denying that Zen practice does not save us from blindness, as the book *Zen at War* demonstrates. Though many I have sat with had measures of dark experiences with teachers before *Zen at War* was published, it was still difficult to read. As an example, it includes these words published in 1934 in Japan from our respected dharma ancestor, Harada Daiun Sogaku:

> The Japanese people are a chosen people whose mission is to control the world. The sword which kills is also the sword which gives life. Comments opposing war are the foolish opinions of those who can only see one aspect of things and not the whole.

> Politics conducted on the basis of a constitution are premature, and therefore fascist politics should be implemented for the next ten years...Similarly, education makes for shallow, cosmopolitan-minded persons. All people of this country should do Zen. That is to say, they should all awake to the Great Way of the Gods. This is Mahayana Zen.

Whatever clarity Harada had about no self, no other, I cannot find consistency with the Three Pure Precepts in these declarations.

Another example comes to mind in thinking about ways to live all the Three Pure Precepts. In the life of Jewish theologian Abraham Joshua Heschel, he began at an early age, studying Jewish orthodoxy and mysticism, writing poetry, and refining his beliefs, practices, and writing. Meanwhile, Hitler came to power in Germany. Heschel fled alone to teach in New York; his family was lost to the death camps.

In this period of his life, Heschel wrote a poem that differed from what we might find in our tradition only in his use of the word "God."

God follows me everywhere—
Spins a net of glances around me,
Shines upon my sightless back like a sun...

God follows me in tramways, in cafes,
Oh, it is only with the back of the pupils
      of one's eyes that one can see how
      secrets ripen, how visions come to be.

Although Heschel remained committed to what in our
language we might call his practice, it wasn't until the 1960s
that he connected religion and politics. He began thinking,
writing, and speaking about civil rights, the needs of the less
fortunate, and opposition to the Vietnam War. He reflected
that few are guilty, but all are responsible. In writings that I
found particularly provocative, he warned that moral apathy
arose from indifference (complacency) and despair. His writings
led to his invitation in 1963 to address a conference titled,
"Religion and Race." To the conferees, Heschel first spoke
of his discomfort with the very name given the conference,
seeing the words "religion" and "race" as contradictory.

> To act in the spirt of religion is to unite what lies
> apart, to remember that humanity as a whole is God's
> beloved child. To act in the spirit of race is to sunder,
> to slash, to dismember the flesh of living humanity...
> Racism is worse than idolatry. Racism is Satanism,
> unmitigated evil.

I would not necessarily use the words *God, religion,* and
race as Heschel did, but I am grateful for his pointer to that
which is here and cannot be divided. I also respect his convic-

tion and willingness to speak his conscience. I think it's likely that he offended many at the conference, since the attendees were there due to their concern for racism. I suspect his words would likely offend people from many perspectives today as well. His words must not have offended Martin Luther King. In 1965 Heschel marched side by side with King in Selma. Deeply moved, Heschel wrote this soon after:

> For many of us the march from Selma to Montgomery was about protest and prayer. Legs are not lips and walking is not kneeling. And yet our legs uttered songs. Even without words, our march was worship. I felt my legs were praying.

Protest and prayer intimately entangled. On that day in 1965, for Heschel walking arose from the entanglement.

The world beckons us to intimacy, with intimacy. Shakyamuni didn't stay seated under the Bodhi Tree after seeing the Venus star. He recognized it; he and the Venus star were and are intimate. Shakyamuni recognized suffering; he and suffering were and are intimate. There was no space between the Venus star rising and speaking the Four Noble Truths.

We are intimate also with our complacency—holding it close—and with despair. We're also intimate with confusion, not knowing what to do. There is no waiting for intimacy, it is here. We are already hopelessly entangled. There is no other way. Carl Jung once said, "If the path before you is clear, you're probably on someone else's."

It seems no religion or endeavor is free from the potential of rigidity and the potential of being complicit in the ethos of our time and place. It is a good thing that we look back at our own lineage and cringe, and that we similarly cringe in looking back at our nation's founders. I can only hope that a future generation will look back at me and us and recognize our limitations. This is what progress looks like, as humanity worldwide has glacially crept toward open heartedness, toward taking up the way of the Precepts. Where rape and pillage by the victor was once the expectation, there is now a court for international war crimes.

Therefore, we need not be deterred from our attempts at living the Precepts, when open hearted and not, when certain and not. Even as we commit to the Ten Grave Precepts, not knowing, too, is our practice.

Once again, here are the Three Pure Precepts:

I vow to maintain the Precepts.

I vow to practice all good dharmas.

I vow to save the many beings.

It's a given, we will get things wrong through action that causes harm intentionally or inadvertently—in violation of the first of the Three Pure Precepts. We will err through inaction by failing to help when we can—in violation of the second. So we sit once again together, and so we take this breath wherever we find ourselves, in commitment to opening to all—living into the third Pure Precept.

12

The permeability of our skin

The whole of our training is for the development of compassion

In *The Path of Compassion,* the writer Christina Feldman relates a story from the Buddha's teachings:

> The Buddha was once asked by a leading disciple, would it be true to say that a part of our training is for the development of love and compassion? The Buddha replied no it would not be true to say this. It would be true to say that the whole of our training is for the development of love and compassion.

"The whole of our training is for the development of love and compassion"—that's a strong statement! But what does it mean?

If Buddha went on to explain, I didn't find record of it. But I do appreciate Zen for its help in our finding the way to meet the world as it is, which is to say, to recognize the world as we are. And I do experience what we call compassion when pierced to any degree by the feeling of another. I recall a time working at a laboratory job with my good friend Bruce when we were in our teens. I touched a hot surface, and at the same instant I cried out in pain, Bruce cried out. In surprise, I looked at him. He said, "I got your vibe." So he did.

Compassion breaks the distinction between self and other. It is the permeability of our skin, not just in profound ways but in the consistent and immediate interactions of our lives. When sitting on a long flight next to a stranger's crying child, we know the difference if our response is an open-hearted *Awww...* or tight-lipped irritation.

I had coffee one morning with someone dear to me— I'll call him Ian—as I was about to write a talk that I wanted to be personal rather than about distant Zen perspectives. I told Ian that I saw him as a caring person, citing just one recent example of his grieving at finding an injured bird on the street and then calling to consult my wife's medical opinion. I asked when compassion worked for him and when it didn't. After pausing for a while, he said he thought he was compassionate as a default but not so much when he was angry. This led to a rich discussion and two stories of his, which I'll share.

Ian lived across the street from a Seattle police station. At three o'clock one morning, he was kept awake by a man standing alone in the middle of the intersection, yelling at the walls of the police station for something done to him or to one he cared about. Ian dressed, went outside, and said to the man that something really disturbing must have happened to him or to someone he loved. He offered the man a soda, whereupon the man calmed down and talked for a few minutes.

Ian didn't ask the man to be quiet nor to let him sleep. He instead touched on things common in the two of them. He also didn't ask for the man's story. I saw these choices as connection with the man and Ian's connection with himself. There was the man, and there was Ian, distinct—like there is sweet and sour. At the same time and without contradiction, there was in that moment one shared humanity, as there is one tongue that tastes sweet and sour, and the existence of sweet that makes sour distinct, and sour makes sweet distinct.

During a different late night, Ian was resting in a parking lot behind a closed business, trying to figure out how to get home. Four police officers were apparently called to the scene, and they were relatively nice to him as they implied they wanted Ian to leave. They asked if he needed anything. "A drink of water would be helpful," Ian said. The officers looked at each other and said they didn't know if they could do that. Was there anything else they could do? Well, a ride to Seattle would be nice. No, they couldn't do that. Both refusals seemed to Ian to be a matter of policy—policy that led to a missed opportunity to bridge police to the one policed, through the sharing of a bottle of water.

I offer both of these stories for their illustration of compassion possible in the smallest human gestures, tones of voice, and presence with another. The gestures are only possible when we meet another as ourselves. That brings us back to the ancient way of Zen and our practice of it today, here.

We quiet our minds in sitting with breath, Mu, and the sensations that are just here. How is this training to develop compassion? Compassion isn't something to pursue, it's what's left when the activity of mind is quiet. That's when we can really see what we see. Our minds tend to be busy keeping us safe in this very dangerous world—a good and necessary thing also, but deadening if always mediating our perception of all that is around us.

Thich Nhat Hanh had great faith in zazen and what would flow from its sincere practice. During a retreat of his that I attended, we participants were encouraged to make a commitment to the Precept of not using intoxicating substances. He said that if we opened our hearts, we'd see the harm caused by alcohol and wouldn't partake at all, even if not at risk ourselves of abuse or even intoxication.

Many of us there didn't share his perspective on that Precept. But his faith in our shared Buddha nature is a gift, an encouragement that I'm still receiving. It's inspiring in part because I trust it was true for him. He didn't ask us to believe his conclusion about the Precept; he asked that we release the concepts that divide us and see anew with our own heart-minds. I share that faith and believe it's true for us all, no matter our path of release. The path of release and the ensuing compassion can be easy to doubt when we observe that it includes unpredictable winding and backtracking. Sometimes there is no straight course to plot. These twists and turns can be harmful to our individual selves and to each other, even as the twists are unavoidable.

Thich Nhat Hanh understood this as shown in this verse within his wonderful poem, "Please Call Me by My True Names":

> I am the twelve-year-old girl,
> refugee on a small boat,
> who throws herself into the ocean
> after being raped by a sea pirate.
> And I am the pirate,
> my heart not yet capable
> of seeing and loving.

Only after returning to his own quiet mind, Nhat Hanh released retribution against the pirates. There is no separation in the words, "And I am the pirate..." In that one phrase, Nhat Hanh is no longer contained by the skin we usually use to define the border of "me." Without setting a linear course for the pirate, faith in Buddha nature abounds in the words, "...not *yet* capable of seeing and loving."

I don't ask anyone to believe this perspective of Buddha nature, the release of concepts, or that compassion will arise of its own. My tears in reading the "true names" poem affirm my own recognition of something valid in what's said. I only ask that if you aren't sure and you want to know if these words carry truth, sit down and let go of ideas of who you are and who you are not.

The images of pirates and the rape of a child are extreme, and there is importance to the scale of the harm caused by a heart not yet open to seeing and loving. Still, in proportion, we can recognize the current characteristics of our own hearts when open and when not. We can bring simple appreciation for the discomfort of it when our hearts cannot open. We can bring that same appreciation for the discomfort in another whose heart is not yet capable of being open in this moment.

These same dynamics of compassion, separation, and engagement are threads through the poems and koan stories that teach us. In a poem cited in Chapter 2, "The form of Zen in relationship," Izumi Shikibu gives us this:

> Although I try
> to hold the single thought
> of Buddha's teaching in my heart,
> I cannot help but hear
> the many crickets' voices calling as well.

Izumi echoes Nhat Hanh's perspective; her sincere meditation led her to hear the voices of the world.

A view of the winding road of zazen and compassion shows up in a koan referenced in this book's Chapter 1, "Everyone we meet is our teacher." In that koan story, there was an old woman who, after caring for a hermit for twenty years, one day asked the seventeen-year-old girl who brought the hermit his daily food to hug him and ask what he felt. He responded: "an old tree on a cold cliff; Midwinter—no warmth." The old woman said he was a vulgar good-for-nothing and kicked him out. In case that left any ambiguity, she burned down the hut.

When discussing this koan in Chapter 1, I asked what response you think would have satisfied the old woman. That's still a worthy question. Today though, you are the hermit who has been supported for twenty years. You've been pretty isolated and done a lot of zazen. A girl surprises you with a hug and asks what you're feeling. What is your response?

I know if what occurred to me to say was "old tree on a cold cliff...no warmth," then my years of zazen had not opened my heart-mind. I don't recognize what I feel, and I'm separate from the girl. Thank you, old woman, for your actions to shake me from what must have been my indifference and alienation. The woman acted on behalf of the Buddha so I can recognize the girl, the hut, the old woman, and myself for what we are.

Speaking for myself, thank you also, hermit, for your teaching about the hindrances to compassion. In your story we recognize ourselves and the ways we may fail to see when we have separated ourselves from someone, everyone, or everything. We can disconnect by numbing ourselves with substances, distractions, and even zazen. We can distance ourselves with pity that declares suffering as yours and not mine. And we can disengage through indifference while focusing on our own needs.

Bringing compassion now, we bow to the fear of loss and pain that motivate us to employ the hindrances of separation. Our compassion can also be impeded by our certainty, righteousness, and anger. In fact, in this unsafe world none of us can escape the use of such hindrances some of the time. Though it would seem safer if we could always act in ways better than that, it is a relief to embrace the truth of who we are.

The emperor of China asked Bodhidharma, "Who is this standing before me?" Bodhidharma said, "I don't know," and left.

The emperor of China could have been angry with Bodhi-dharma when he asked who this was standing before him. Implied in the question: That Bodhidharma was not the emperor. In responding, "I don't know," Bodhidharma didn't say his name and didn't deny his name. He stepped aside from declaring one or separate, leaving all open.

You are the emperor of China. Who is this that stands before you now?

In another time of my life, I was a principal in the Society of Automotive Engineers Fire Safety Committee. Meetings and conferences were environments with as practical a focus as any, using objective measurements and tools as much as possible. At the meeting were consultants who supported plaintiffs in suing auto manufacturers for injurious fires they believed were preventable. There were engineers from auto manufacturers and consultants who supported manufacturers in defense against those lawsuits, arguing that not all fires are preventable. And there were representatives of manufacturers of prevention technology, such as fire retardants and fire sup-pression systems.

Everyone was knowledgeable of and committed to vehicle fire safety—a laudable issue. To give a flavor of meetings, one might argue that a fire could have been prevented by an inex-pensive part judiciously placed. Another might agree and com-plain there was no end to the addition of parts that could be added for the next crash occurring at another angle or faster driving speed, with no place to draw a line of enough.

Yet all were in the same room, blundering along to improve safety and influence policy. As each of us had our area of expertise and concern, we all lived within one world, indivisibly connected.

The undercurrents and closed hearts were part of the progress, and indeed fire safety improved over time as studies were done and compromises made. Before grim conclusions about the species are drawn, note one statistic: Whether in spite of, independent of, or because of this chaos, vehicle fires per miles driven decreased steadily by 81 percent from 1980 to 2018.

Founding Zen teachers of our own lineage, humans all, demonstrated times and ways their hearts were not yet open to seeing and loving. Let me lay out a couple of generations of the Three Treasures Sangha lineage for context, then I'll give some background on two of the founders.

Harada Daiun Sogaku was the teacher of Yasutani Roshi. Yasutani went on to found the Sanbo Kyodan line, a Japanese tradition unusually supportive of lay practice. Sanbo Kyodan translates as "the three treasures," leading to the name of the group I now sit with, Three Treasures Sangha of the Pacific Northwest. Yasutani Roshi gave transmission to Yamada Kōun Roshi, who in turn gave transmission to Robert Aitken, and Aitken to my teacher, Jack Duffy.

Harada was a respected teacher with training in both Soto and Rinzai traditions. Many of the teachers in the U.S. you may know trace back to Harada and Yasutani. In 1934, Harada wrote that the Japanese people were chosen, their mission was to control the world, that fascist politics should be implemented for the next ten years, and that all Japanese people should study Zen.

Before seeking our own response to such beliefs in our lineage, let's look also at similarities in the beliefs of his student, Yasutani. In February 2000, Kubota Ji'un, as the third abbot of the Sanbo Kyodan line, published an apology about the behavior of the lineage founder, Yasutani. In the letter of apology, Kubota Ji'un Roshi confirmed the strong right-wing and antisemitic beliefs held by Yasutani during and after WWII. He also said:

> ...Yamada Kōun Roshi, who was to take over as the second abbot, admonished Yasutani Roshi more than a few times for the latter's ideological inclination, and reminded him of the initial responsibility of concentrating upon the reviving of the pure Dharma, the intrinsic core of Buddhism.

Pause for a moment and take stock of your own heart—open and closed. This too is a call to compassion. Zen is valuable in the good times and essential in challenging times—times of doubt and anger, aversion and fear. What does nonseparation mean in hearing these stories of our ancestors—nonseparation from them, from ourselves, and from Zen?

For me, the stories of teachings of these ancestors have been part of my own Zen training for years. I am grateful for the gifts of the practice they've fostered for me and the world, and I respect the wisdom of their Zen teaching. I'm shocked by the suffering and death they've contributed to in the name of this same practice. I have to conclude that all of us are subject to such times, and no individual is wise enough to escape ignorance and harm that can propagate for generations.

Take stock of your own heart, open or closed. It's natural to rail and blame him, her, and them, just as it's natural to recognize our own behavior and respond with shame, railing at ourselves. Is there another way?

I have a nephew who was friendly with a doctor in the Rwandan health facility in which my nephew was doing a fellowship after college. The two would warmly greet each other in passing, and they sometimes talked casually. One day my nephew learned this doctor had worked in a major hospital during the genocide against the Tutsis and in his position, he identified all the Tutsi patients to be killed. My nephew described a confusing discord in his sense of reality—a friendly killer, one person.

If we can see Harada of fascist activism and Harada as a strict teacher who fostered Zen across the world—and Harada as me and as you—then we find the permeability of our skin. This is a story from the formidable Japanese teacher Hakuin, from *Zen Flesh, Zen Bones:*

> A soldier named Nobushige came to Hakuin, and asked: "Is there really a paradise and a hell?" "Who are you?" inquired Hakuin. "I am a samurai," the warrior replied. "You, a soldier!" exclaimed Hakuin. "What kind of ruler would have you as his guard? Your face looks like that of a beggar." Nobushige became so angry that he began to draw his sword, but Hakuin continued: "So you have a sword! Your weapon is probably much too dull to cut off my head." As Nobushige drew his sword

Hakuin remarked: "Here open the gates of hell!" At these words the samurai, perceiving the master's discipline, sheathed his sword and bowed. "Here open the gates of paradise," said Hakuin.

In Hakuin's speaking those six words, "Here open the gates of hell!" the moment turned for Nobushige. Before those words, Hakuin was the enemy to be destroyed. After those words, Nobushige joined Hakuin with a bow. Those six words are meant for me and you. We know what to do when the gates of hell are open—reverently bow to this too. This is zazen. The story doesn't share what happened after the bow. That next response, the actualization of zazen, is open to us right now.

My caring friend Ian expressed it pretty clearly when he said his default was to recognize the feelings of others such that a caring response arose, and this same pathway was sometimes clouded by anger and contempt. The same dynamic is within and without; when recognizing ourselves, a caring response arises. When our perception of ourselves is clouded by shame and comparisons, caring responses are hindered. There is room for a caring response when there is no denial of blindness to ourselves and others that causes harm.

Philosophies and beliefs about right and wrong are subject to error. Start here.

Zazen is meeting it all with permeable skin. I am Yasutani Roshi, and I played a part in war and in a path of peace. I am sad now thinking of one part and grateful for the chance of the other. I am a Jew, closely connected to men and women still wounded by concentration camps. And I live a life of means beyond most people in the world. I don't know unambiguous rules by which to judge, and yet I live life.

There are ethical systems that can help, and then at some point a choice is made. But who is there to make a choice? Bodhidharma said, "I don't know." The one who decides is not the one who parses and defines. I have found I can trust the quiet mind before words and evaluations. Please, see for yourself.

13
Always in relationship

The oak tree in the courtyard

In this final chapter, it seems fitting to emphasize the fundamental fact of our undying relationship to pen and paper, teacup, lips, and throat. After chapters filled with words, consider this story from *The Gateless Barrier* about the teacher Chao-chou:

> A monk asked Chao-chou, "What is the meaning of Bodhidharma coming from the west?"
> Chao-chou said, "The oak tree in the courtyard."

Chao-chou steers the monk away from principles and toward a specific tree that he can see and touch. This isn't a diversion or avoidance of the question—it is a cogent response. We can talk about relationship in endless lovely ways that will distance us from it unless we take the point from our worthy ancestor.

Also from *The Gateless Barrier*, Wu-men, the compiler of the koan collection, adds a verse to amplify the direction conveyed by Chao-chou:

Words do not convey the fact;
Language is not an expedient.
Attached to words, your life is lost;
blocked by phrases, you are bewildered.

Words are essential, though it helps to be clear of their role. Words are metaphors, symbols alluding to the fact but not able to fully convey it. I can tell you it's windy where I am today, and you will understand something of it. You won't know whether it's strong enough to create a roaring sound in my ears. "Windy" doesn't communicate that I can't see the wind through the window; what I do see across the span of my field of view are laurel leaves, oak leaves, and cedar boughs moving up and down, right and left, changing light and shadow as they do. The seeing is not the description of seeing. Describing a difference between "direct experience" and words and concepts doesn't help.

To say we're "in relationship" is also ambiguous. Do we mean there is me and there is the oak tree? Or there is me and there is you? "In relationship" can also allude to the intimate joining of me and oak, leaving only oak. All our koans use words to point beyond them, to see, to hear, to recognize the elemental again. Chao-chou redirects the monk away from trying to figure it out.

In seventeenth-century Japan, Bashō knew that intimate joining was necessary to have the clarity to write a poem. His student, Hattori Toho, first quoted his old teacher and then explained the meaning with respect to writing poetry.

I'll reprise the quotation cited in Chapter 2, "The form of Zen in relationship":

> "Learn about the pine from the pine, learn about the bamboo from the bamboo." This dictum of our teacher means that you must forgo your subjectivity. If you interpret "learn" in your own way, you will end up not learning. To "learn" here means to enter the object; then if its essence reveals itself and moves you, you may come up with a verse.

As a young man, I remember walking down the hall in my family home and looking toward the screen door when a robin flashed through my field of vision of the yard. With wings spread, it appeared from the right and crossed out of sight to the left. For that one moment, there was the shock of red feathers and no thought of where I was walking to or why. There was nothing special about me or seeing the robin in that second or two.

I suspect we all have those moments. Ikkyū wrote about one such moment for him:

> A Gentleman's Wealth
>
> A poet's treasure consists of words and phrases;
> A scholar's days and nights are perfumed with book.
> For me, plum blossoms framed by the window is
>   an unsurpassable pleasure;
> A stomach tight with cold, but still enchanted
>   by snow, the moon, and dawn frost

Ours is a practice of being available to see what we see, to hear what we hear. With a quiet(er) mind we are graced with more such moments, and moments that can stretch into minutes and beyond. Ikkyū did not leave out aching cold when enchanted by snow and moon. The aching cold was framed by the same window, holding its own bitter enchantment.

In the course of a day, we see, then dream, and then see again. My friend Myra once told me of a typical workday in a senior center. Sometimes she could walk behind someone shuffling down the narrow hall and comfortably match pace, just taking the pace as is. Other times, walking behind the same woman as she methodically stepped and reset her walker, Myra would do a little dance—legs moving faster up and down, though not able to propel her forward any faster.

This too is relationship to woman and walker, plum blossom and dawn frost. We are in relationship within the world we meet. It sounds simple, though we know it can be unusual for us to relax into only this right here. Instead of being in the hall with the elderly woman and walker, our mind naturally flies away to the urgent phone call to be made or the care needed of another in the room ahead. When our minds have flown ahead, our bodies are still in step with woman and walker, but we have lost our recognition of that together-ness. Flown-ahead mind too is in the field of view, just another oak tree.

One translator cited the following as a poem written by Ikkyū after his enlightenment at hearing a crow while he was meditating on a boat in a lake:

For twenty years I was in a turmoil
Seething and angry, but now my time has come!
The crow laughs, an arhat emerges from the filth,
And in the sunlight a jade beauty sings!

It seems Ikkyū held ideas of awakening and not awakening, and maybe of self and no self until seeing through years and pride. And so he saw what was left: Everything. *"Caaawww!"* The filth wasn't extinguished, and it did not block the sun from illuminating the jade.

As a gift to us, Ikkyū continued to write poems that included the crow. Each one was new, immediate, still intimate with crow and more. In this first one, Ikkyū continues to relish the night on Lake Biwa:

one pause between each crow's reckless shriek
Ikkyū Ikkyū Ikkyū

Any experience we have is immediate and, if not constrained by our conclusions, becomes newly mixed with life today and memories alive in us, as we can see in this poem from Ikkyū:

ten dumb years I wanted things to be different
furious proud I still feel it
one summer midnight in my little boat on Lake Biwa
caaaawwweeeee
father when I was a boy you left us now I forgive you

Talking about it like this raises more ways to want things to be different, so it's up to me and you to simply recognize what's left. When dust-mopping the living room, threads of dust from under the couch are lighter than the air disturbed by the mop, rising and turning, even as I chase them. Naming it "dust," I chase it, intent on capturing it to protect the house. When seeing through, dust, living room, floor, air, and mop dance in a single motion, mutually responsive. Insignificant, and yet each plays a part. To say each substance is in relationship is already saying too much, bounding each as separate from the other. One dance holding steady is like speaking Spanish as a second language without translating in my mind before speaking—engaged, yet it's just speaking, nothing special. Still, I'm pretty happy about it when it happens.

There is no escape from the call of the crow; you are on Lake Biwa and the *caaawww caaawww* completely fills space and time. Where in the piercing sound is a beak? In fact, where in that *caaawww* is your own mouth? Don't let such questions pull you from the *caaawww* or the darkness.

I can't help but think that Ikkyū wouldn't have been pleased with one translator's description that he was "meditating" in the boat; he refused to allow a description to fog the ordinary totality of a moment:

> sick of it whatever it's called sick of the names
> I dedicate every pore to what's here

Ikkyū was irreverent and shameless in his authenticity, impatient with administration of Zen temples and restrictions of social norms. He was as vehement in avoiding the staleness of his own enlightenment experience:

the crow's *caw* was ok but one night with a
lovely whore opened a wisdom deeper than
what the bird said

Dedicating every pore to what's here includes names, but avoids being limited by them such that we miss the unnamable. If I tell a story that includes reference to Davis, my daughter's dog, no one will know that he sensually sleeps like a cat in a patch of afternoon sun on the top edge of the couch. If I doubt the validity of my fatigue, I may believe in my laziness—until learning I have a fever and the flu, and then permitting myself to go to bed.

Dedicated to what's here—Davis or fatigue—there is no question, no doubt, and no need to validate.

I received my first koan from Joshu Sasaki Roshi at sesshin at Jemez Bodhi Mandala in New Mexico: "Who am I when looking at the pine tree?"

Sasaki patiently met me each dokusan (one-to-one meeting with a teacher), straightening his spine, arms on each side at angles about thirty degrees from the vertical. He was inviting me to see through one seeing a pine tree, to see this pine tree of wood and needles, filtering light and casting shade. No such luck for me that long week.

Thich Nhat Hanh described interconnectedness, inter-being, in real-life terms. Sun warms the earth; plants and animals grow. None of them are independent. If we trace the life of the produce upon which we rely, we are likely to find transportation reliant on energy and requiring manufacture, and all kinds of people—those with whom we agree and those with whom we disagree. All are in the web of mutual support: Food to us, a living for them. We can understand this indivisible web of connection. To experience it takes something different.

Each day in our sutra service, we chant these lines from Daio Kokushi's "On Zen":

> O my good worthy friends gathered here,
> If you desire to listen to the thunderous voice
>   of the Dharma,
> Exhaust your words, empty your thoughts,
> For then you may come to recognize
>   this one essence.

Our ancestors are consistently steering us in one direction: Exhaust your words, empty your thoughts. We can conveniently describe the means of doing so as "zazen," though I know people whose zazen is running, with marathons providing an intentionality similar to sesshin. I know people whose zazen is practicing guitar, playing each note with fingers and string, ears and instrument. Let's not limit our own responses to our ancestors by the words we and they use.

"Zazen" is not a word, or at least not only a word. Zazen is an embrace of the world, not despite anything we could list, but because of everything—tears and laughter, love and hate.

Zazen is not in an argument with what is, it is living into this one life we have.

Zazen is not a passive acceptance, but an active response to just this.

Zazen is not an esoteric practice to be done at given times of the day, but participation now with the person in the grocery store line and the plane overhead. Without an idea of a participant, only person and plane are left.

You know what to do.

References

Sutras and Precepts

Arrow Sallattha Sutta
   Translated by Thanissaro Bhikkhu.
   https://bit.ly/ArrowSutra

Diamond Sangha Sutras
   Translated by Robert Aitken. Used by permission via
   Honolulu Diamond Sangha correspondence.

Sutra book of the Three Treasures Sangha of the Pacific
   Northwest (Diamond Sangha lineage)
   Translated by Robert Aitken; "The Four Vows"
   translated by Jack Duffy.

Books

Aeschylus, *The House of Atreus; Being the Agamemnon, the
   Libation Bearers, and the Furies.* Translated by E.D.A.
   Morshead. Norwalk, CT: Easton Press, 1979.
   [See also Robert F. Kennedy misquote at
   https://bit.ly/RFKquote]

Aitken, Robert, commentary and translation, *Encouraging
   Words: Zen Buddhist Teachings for Western Students.*
   San Francisco and New York: Pantheon Books, 1993.

_____, *The Gateless Barrier: The Wu-Men Kuan.* San Francisco: North Point Press, 1990.

Basho: The Complete Haiku. Translated by Jane Reichhold. New York: Kodansha, 2013.

_____, *The Moon in the Pines: Zen Haiku.* Selected and translated Jonathan Clements. New York: Viking Studio, 2000.

Beck, Charlotte Joko, *Nothing Special: Living Zen.* New York: HarperCollins, 1993.

Chao-Chou, *The Recorded Sayings of Zen Master Joshu.* Translated by James Green. Boulder, CO: Shambhala, 2001.

Cook, Francis Dojun, *How to Raise an Ox: Zen Practice as Taught in Master Dōgen's Shobogenzo.* Somerville, MA: Wisdom Publications, 2011.

Dōgen, Eihei, *Dōgen's Extensive Record: A Translation of the Eihei Kōroku.* Translated by and edited by Taigen Dan Leighton. Somerville, MA: Wisdom Publication, 2004.

_____, *The True Dharma Eye: Zen Master Dōgen's Three Hundred Koans.* Translated by Kazuaki Tanahashi and John Daido Loori. Boulder, CO: Shambala, 2005.

_____, *The Zen Poetry of Dōgen: Verses from the Mountain of Eternal Peace.* Translated by Steven Heine. Rutland, VT: Tuttle Publishing, 1997.

Dongshan Liangjie, *Encounter Dialogues of Dongshan Liangjie.* Translated by Chang Chung-yuan. Compiled by Satyavayu. Hungary: Terebess Center, 2013. https://bit.ly/DongshanDialogues

_____, *The Record of Tung-shan Classics in East Asian Buddhism.* Translated by Liang-chieh and William F. Powell. Honolulu, HI: University of Hawaii Press, 1986. https://bit.ly/TungshanClassics

Feldman, Christina, et al., "Nurturing Compassion," *The Path of Compassion.* San Francisco, CA: Parallax Press, 1988.

Heschel, Abraham Joshua, *The Sabbath.* New York: Farrar Straus Giroux, 2005.

Hirshfield, Jane, *Nine Gates: Entering the Mind of Poetry.* New York: HarperCollins, 1997.

Hongzhi, *Cultivating the Empty Field: The Silent Illumination of Zen Master Hongzhi.* Translated by Taigen Dan Leighton and YiWu. Rutland, VT: Tuttle Publishing, 2000.

Huston, Matt, "Loneliness: A New Epidemic in the USA," *Psychology Today,* February 12, 2019. https://bit.ly/HustonLoneliness

Ikkyū: Crow With No Mouth: 15th Century Zen Master. Translated by Stephen Berg. Port Townsend, WA: Copper Canyon Press, 2000.

_____, *Wild Ways: Zen Poems of Ikkyū.* Translated by John Stevens. Lake View, NY: White Pine Press, 2007.

Izumi Shikibu, "Although I try...," *The Ink Dark Moon: Love Poems by Onono Komachi and Izumi Shikibu.* Translated by Jane Hirshfield and Mariko Aratani. New York: Vintage Books, 1990.

Jinniu, "Case 74: Jinniu's Rice Pail," *The Blue Cliff Record.* Translated by Yamada Kōun, Robert Aitken, and Nelson Foster, with revisions and Pinyin transliteration by Michael Kieran. Honolulu Diamond Sangha, 2008.

Kabir: Ecstatic Poems. Translated by Robert Bly. Boston, MA: Beacon Press, 1977.

Keizan, *Transmission of Light: Zen in the Art of Enlightenment by Zen Master Keizan.* Translated by Thomas Cleary. New York: North Point Press, 1990.

Kokushi, Daiō, "On Zen," *Manual of Zen Buddhism.* Edited and translated by D.T. Suzuki. Buddha Dharma Education Association, 2005 (original author copyright, 1935). https://bit.ly/kokushBuddhanet

Kubota Ji'un, "Apology for What the Founder of the Sanbo Kyodan, Yasutani Haku'un Roshi, Said and Did During World War II." Translated by Satô M. February 2000. https://bit.ly/thezensiteaplogy

Li Po [Li Bai], "Zazen on Ching-t'ing Mountain," *Crossing the Yellow River: Three Hundred Poems from the Chinese.* Translated by Sam Hamill. Rochester: BOA Editions Ltd., 2000. https://bit.ly/LiPoHamill

Maimonides, Moses, *A Guide for the Perplexed.* Translated by M. Friedländer. New York: E.P. Dutton, 1904. https://bit.ly/Maimonides-Guide

Merton, Thomas, *Thomas Merton: In My Own Words.* Edited by Jonathan Montaldo. Liguori, MO: Liguori Publications, 2007.

_____, *Thoughts in Solitude.* New York: Farrar, Straus & Cudahy, 1998.

Nhat Hanh, Thich, *Call Me By My True Names: The Collected Poems of Thich Nhat Hanh*. Berkeley: Parallax Press, 1999.

Pomerance, Bernard, *The Elephant Man, A Play*. New York: Grove Press, 1979.

Raboteau, Albert J., *American Prophets: Seven Religious Radical & Their Struggle for Social and Political Justice*. Princeton, NJ: Princeton University Press, 2018.

Red Pine (writing as Bill Porter), *The Road to Heaven: Encounters with Chinese Hermits*. New York: Counterpoint Press, 2009.

_____, *Three Zen Sutras: The Heart, The Diamond, and The Platform Sutras*. New York: Counterpoint Press, 2021.

Reps, Paul and Nyogen Senzaki, *Zen Flesh, Zen Bones: A Collection of Zen and Pre-Zen Writings*. North Clarentdon, VT: Tuttle Publishing, 1998.

Roberts, Elizabeth and Elias Amidon, *Earth Prayers: 365 Prayers, Poems, and Invocations from Around the World*, 1991. San Francisco, CA: HarperOne, 2009.

Ryōkan, *One Robe, One Bowl: The Zen Poetry of Ryōkan*. Translated by John Stevens. Boulder, CO: Shambhala Publications, 1977.

Sasaki, Ruth F. (translator), and Thomas Yuho Kirchner (editor), *The Record of Linji* (University of Hawaii Press, 2009).

Shitou Xiqian, "The Tallying of Difference and Sameness." Translated by Nelson Foster. Permission via personal correspondence, 2023.

Shōji, *The Eastern Buddhist*, vol. 5, no. 1, May 1972. Translated by Norman Waddell, Abe Masao, Genjō kōan. https://bit.ly/ShojiJSTOR

Stonehouse, *The Mountain Poems of Stonehouse*. Translated by Red Pine. Port Townsend, WA: Copper Canyon Press, 2014.

The Blue Cliff Record. Translated by Thomas Cleary and J.C. Cleary Boulder, CO: Shambhala, 1992.

The Entangling Vines: A Classic Collection of Zen Koans. Edited and translated by Thomas Yuho Kirchner. Somerville, MA: Wisdom Publications, 2013.

Trejo, Danny, *Trejo: My Life of Crime, Redemption, and Hollywood*. New York: Atria Books, 2022.

Tutu, Desmond M., *No Future Without Forgiveness*. New York: Image, Doubleday, 2000.

Victoria, Brian Daizen, *Zen at War*, 2nd edition. Lanham, MD: Rowman & Littlefield, 2006.

Wiesenthal, Simon, *The Sunflower: On the Possibilities and Limits of Forgiveness*. New York: Schocken Books, 2008. [Includes Jean Améry, "At the Mind's Limits: Contemplations by a Survivor on Auschwitz and Its Realities."]

Specific Citations

Epigraph

Although I try / to hold the single thought...
  Izumi Shikubu, *The Ink Dark Moon,* p. 139.

The teacher said, "Don't think good; don't think evil..."
  Aitken, *The Gateless Barrier*, p. 147.

1: Everyone we meet is our teacher

Chü-chih and True World
  Aitken, *The Gateless Barrier,* p. 29.

Case 154: There was an old woman who supported a hermit...
  Kirchner, *The Entangling Vines,* p. 20.

2: The form of Zen in relationship

[A] student said to Master [Ikkyū], "Please write for me..."
  Beck, *Nothing Special: Living Zen,* p. 168.

Although I try / to hold the single thought...
  Izumi Shikubu, *The Ink Dark Moon,* p. 139.

The birds have vanished down the sky...
  Li Po, "Zazen on Ching-t'ing Mountain."
  Online at https://bit.ly/LiPoHamill

Learn about the pine from the pine...
Hattori Toh; Hirshfield, trans.; *Nine Gates*, p. 101.

[Romeo] does not care for Juliet...
Pomerance, *The Elephant Man, A Play*, 1979.

3: Contemplation and engagement are not separate

Driven to find how to live in this world...
Author's retelling.

If our life is poured out in useless words...
Merton, *Thoughts in Solitude*, p. 91.

I make monastic silence a protest against the lies...
Merton, *In My Own Words*, p. 82.

One day before noon, the Bhagavan put on...
Red Pine, *Three Zen Sutras*, pp. 11–13.

A number of monks then came up to where...
Red Pine, *Three Zen Sutras*, pp. 11–13.

Bring to rest the thoughts of the ceaselessly seeking mind...
Sasaki, *The Record of Linji*, p. 7.

Since there is nothing to attain, the Bodhisattva lives by...
From sutras used by the Three Treasures Sangha.

So nowadays please do not acquiesce to sages...
Hongzhi, *Cultivating the Empty Field*, pp. 54–55.

Truly is anything missing now?...
Hakuin, in Aitken, *Encouraging Words*, p. 180.

Though there be the purity of the autumn waters...
Keizan, *Transmission of the Light*, p. 27.

4: Hermits and householders

Some retired to achieve their ideals; some bowed out...
Red Pine, *Road to Heaven,* p. 24.

...when Ch'u Yuan was banished he wandered along rivers...
Red Pine, *Road to Heaven,* pp. 25–26.

Contemplating your own authentic form is how to...
Cheng-chüeh, *Cultivating the Empty Field,* p. 38.

In visions of the night, like dropping rain...
Aeschylus, *Agamemnon* in *The House of Atreus.*

One day before noon, the Bhagavan put on...
Red Pine, *Three Zen Sutras,* pp. 11–13.

...and the fisherman said a sage isn't bothered by others...
Red Pine, *Road to Heaven,* pp. 25–26.

I alone am clean everyone is drunk I alone am sober...
Red Pine, *Road to Heaven,* pp. 25–26.

...if the world is muddy splash in the mire...
Red Pine, *Road to Heaven,* pp. 25–26.

If you can experience yourself without distractions...
Cheng-chüeh, *Cultivating the Empty Field,* p. 38.

There is a realm of time where the goal is not to have...
Heschel, *The Sabbath,* p. 3.

5: Practicing together with suffering

A monk asked Tung Shan, "When cold and heat come..."
Cleary, trans., *The Blue Cliff Record,* p. 258.

A woman stumbles off a cliff, and midway down...
Author's text.

Tung Shan said, "When it's cold, the cold kills you...
  Cleary, trans., *The Blue Cliff Record,* p. 258.

...Pain...falls drop by drop upon the heart...
  Robert F. Kennedy [mis]quoting Aeschylus.
  Online at https://bit.ly/RFKquote

[Job] 3:20 Wherefore is light given to him...
  From the Hebrew Bible.

...soon to die yet showing no sign in the cicada's voice...
  Basho: The Complete Haiku, p. 165.

My God, why hast thou forsaken me?
  Mark 15:34.

Ch'ing asked, "What is the sound outside the gate?"...
  Cleary, trans., *The Blue Cliff Record,* pp. 275–276.

...in emptiness there is...no suffering...
  From the Diamond Sangha Sutras.

Bam. When it hit me, the boogeyman was gone...
  Trejo*: My Life of Crime, Redemption...,* p. 14.

6: Loneliness without separation

Loneliness / In the blue sky a winter goose cries...
  Ryōkan, *One Robe, One Bowl,* p. 53.

In all the findings, a lack of meaningful human connectedness...
  Huston, "Loneliness: A New Epidemic in the USA."
  Online at https://bit.ly/HustonLoneliness

Sun level with the ground. The second hour of the day...
  Chao-Chou, *The Recorded Sayings of Zen Master
  Joshu,* p. 524.

Monks, an uninstructed run-of-the-mill person feels feelings...
From the Arrow Sallattha Sutra.
Online at https://bit.ly/ArrowSutra

So...[the uninstructed run-of-the-mill person] feels two pains...
From the Arrow Sallattha Sutra.
Online at https://bit.ly/ArrowSutra

my friend's funeral this morning...
Ikkyu: Crow with no Mouth, pp. 38.

I was like an old leafless tree...
Ikkyu: Crow with no Mouth, pp. 66.

turn this way! I too feel lonely late in autumn...
Basho: The Complete Haiku, p. 165.

In the very midst of light, there's darkness...
Shitou Xiqian, Nelson Foster, trans. "The Tallying of
Difference and Sameness." Personal correspondence
with the translator.

7: The practice of mutual support

When Linji was one of the assembly of monks...
Sasaki, *The Record of Linji,* p. 50–51.

Zazen is not a practice of isolation...
Aitken, *Encouraging Words,* p. 11.

Linji came back and said to the head monk...
Sasaki, *The Record of Linji,* p. 30–31.

Linji arrived at Dayu's temple...
Sasaki, *The Record of Linji,* p. 51.

Every day, before the midday meal, Master Jinniu...
Yamada Kōun et al., "Case 74: Jinniu's Rice Pail," from
Honolulu Diamond Sangha.

8: The koan of groups

The body is the Bodhi Tree...
Aitken, *The Gateless Barrier,* p. 29.

Bodhi really has no tree; the mirror too has no stand...
Aitken, *The Gateless Barrier,* p. 29.

The Sixth Ancestor was pursued by Ming the head monk...
Aitken, *The Gateless Barrier,* p. 147.

Even if Hui-neng wrote a lovely poem...
Author's text.

Just as one might feel compelled to join...
Author's text.

If seen by day, A firefly Is just a red-necked bug...
Bashō, *The Moon in the Pines,* p. 33.

Are you looking for me? I am in the next seat...
Kabir: Ecstatic Poems, p. 33.

Apprehend God in all things, for God is in all things...
Meister Eckhart, in Roberts et al., *Earth Prayers,* p. 251.

9: Hurt, anger, forgiveness, and acceptance

Nanyang arrived at the front of the palace...
Dōgen, *The True Dharma Eye,* p. 205.

Blind passions without cease, I vow to see through.
From sutras used by the Three Treasures Sangha.

Delusion is inexhaustible; I vow to cut it off....
From Diamond Sangha Sutras.

Greed, anger, and ignorance rise endlessly; I vow to abandon them.
From Diamond Sangha Sutras.

Greed, hatred, and ignorance rise endlessly; I vow to abandon them.
From Diamond Sangha Sutras.

All the evil karma, ever created by me since of old...
From Diamond Sangha Sutras.

...on account of my beginningless greed, hatred and ignorance...
Aitken, *Encouraging Words*, p. 170.

The officer said, "Behind the windows of the second floor..."
Wiesenthal, *The Sunflower*, pp. 42-43.

If I had been in such a situation, perhaps I would have...
Améry, in Wiesenthal, *The Sunflower*, pp. 106–107.

All the evil karma, ever created by me since of old...
Aitken, *Encouraging Words*, p. 170.

My humanity is inextricably bound up in yours...
Tutu, *No Future Without Forgiveness*, p. 31.

10: Why does it come to this?

One time when the Master was washing his bowls...
Dongshan, *The Record of Tung-shan Classics*.
Online https://bit.ly/TungshanClassics

All beings beyond number, I vow to free.
From sutras used by the Three Treasures Sangha.

The many beings are numberless; I vow to save them.
From Diamond Sangha Sutras.

Once when Master Dongshan was washing his bowls...
Dongshan, *Encounter Dialogues of Dongshan Liangjie*.
Online at https://bit.ly/DongshanDialogues

Scorpion tails and wolf hearts pervade the world...
Stonehouse, *The Mountain Poems of Stonehouse,* p. 43.

...a monk asked Yün-men, "How is it when it is expressed..."
Dōgen, *Dōgen's Extensive Record,* p. 160.

The many beings are numberless, I vow to save them.
From Diamond Sangha Sutras.

If you make a vow not to see a woman for ages...
Cook, *How to Raise an Ox,* pp. 105–107.

When one thing becomes a Buddha...
Cook, *How to Raise an Ox,* p. 85.

You only attain the mind of Buddha when...
Shōji, *The Eastern Buddhist,* pp. 79–80.
Online at https://bit.ly/ShojiJSTOR

What can I accomplish?...
Dōgen, *The Zen Poetry of Dōgen,* poem 22-J.

11: Engaging the Precepts

I take up the Way of Not Killing. [Ten Grave Precepts]
From Diamond Sangha Sutras.

I vow to maintain the Precepts. [Three Pure Precepts]
From Diamond Sangha Sutras.

The Japanese people are a chosen people...
Victoria, *Zen at War,* p. 137.

God follows me everywhere...
Raboteau, *American Prophets,* p. 6.

To act in the spirt of religion is to unite...
Raboteau, *American Prophets,* p. 6.

For many of us the march from Selma to Montgomery...
Raboteau, *American Prophets,* p. 6.

12: The permeability of our skin

The Buddha was once asked by a leading disciple...
Feldman, *The Path of Compassion,* p. 19.

I am the twelve-year-old girl, refugee on a small boat...
Nhat Hanh, *Call Me By My True Names,* p. 63–64.

Although I try / to hold the single thought...
Izumi Shikubu, *The Ink Dark Moon,* p. 139.

Yamada Kōun Roshi, who was to take over as...
Kubota Ji'un, "Apology for What the Founder of the
Sanbo Kyodan..."
Online at https://bit.ly/thezensiteaplogy

A soldier named Nobushige came to Hakuin...
Reps, *Zen Flesh, Zen Bones,* p. 46.

13: Always in relationship

A monk asked Chao-chou, "What is the meaning of..."
Aitken, *The Gateless Barrier,* p. 226.

Words do not convey the fact; Language is not an expedient...
Aitken, *The Gateless Barrier,* p. 226.

Learn about the pine from the pine...
Hattori Toho, in Hirshfield, trans., *Nine Gates,* p. 101.

A Gentleman's Wealth—A poet's treasure consists of...
Ikkyū, *Wild Ways: Zen Poems of Ikkyū,* p. 42.

For twenty years I was in a turmoil...
Ikkyū, *Wild Ways: Zen Poems of Ikkyū,* p. ix.

one pause between each crow's reckless shriek...
Ikkyu: Crow With No Mouth, p. 51.

ten dumb years I wanted things to be different...
Ikkyu: Crow With No Mouth, p. 42.

sick of it whatever it's called sick of the names...
Ikkyu: Crow With No Mouth, p. 56.

the crow's *caw* was ok but one night...
Ikkyu: Crow With No Mouth, p. 58.

O my good worthy friends gathered here...
Kokushi, *Manual of Zen Buddhism,* p. 100.
Online at https://bit.ly/kokushBuddhanet